louis armstrong

To Woody Allen, who delights in Satchmo

First published in The United States of America in 1998 by
RIZZOLI INTERNATIONAL PUBLICATIONS, INC.
300 Park Avenue South, New York, NY 10010

First published in France in 1998 by
Éditions Plume
2, rue de la Roquette
Cour Sainte-Marguerite
75011 Paris

ISBN 0-8478-2131-5
LC 98-65883

Translated by Charles Penwarden
Design by Jean-Yves Verdu, Paris

Special thanks to: Jean-Luc Andrieu, George Avakian,
Dominique Bernard, Claude Carrière, Nicole Colomb, Irakli
de Davrichewy, Daniel Richard, Joan Dean, Frank Ténot,
Philippe Carles, Genneviève Stewart and Louis Comte and
the following issues: Jazz Magazine, Cahiers du Jazz, Jazz-Hot,
Bulletin du Hot Club de France, Métronome, Down Beat,
Melody Maker, Time, Jazz Journal, Record Research, The
Record Changer

Printed in Italy

louis armstrong

michel boujut

RIZZOLI
NEW YORK

Interview with Wynton Marsalis

Katherine Adzima What did the trumpet sound like before Louis Armtrong? What did he do to it?

Wynton Marsalis He freed all of the music from the performance conventions of the day, and he made it more human and natural. Not just the playing of the trumpet and the singing, but music in general because musicians on every instrument imitated him. His way of phrasing, the way he took the blues and applied the sound and the feeling of the blues to traditional harmony, like the harmony of Schubert. And there is his whole persona, which is a combination of respect and irreverence, which is one of the essentials of the American character.... Eventually people started having whole bands that sounded like him. Duke Ellington once said that he wanted to hear people on every instrument play like Louis Armstrong.

KA And he was also the first singer to scat. You said that he used his voice in the same way that he used his trumpet.

WM Yes. People scatted in New Orleans and he was the first to record scatting, but his real contribution to vocal styling is the way of phrasing. The freedom, the ease of phrasing. His phrasing is not stilted by the music. Whenever you're singing, you're worrying about the pitches and whether you're in tune ... and the rhythms. Louis Armstrong had perfect pitch, he was always in tune. And he also possessed the greatest degree of rhythmic sophistication, so it allowed him a certain freedom in dealing with the music. And he took that freedom, he took that liberty—and everybody tried to imitate him, from Billie Holiday to Frank Sinatra.

KA Louis died when you were about ten. Did you ever get to see him?

WM No. I didn't respect him when I was ten. I was a typical American—didn't respect anything—just from another generation, really. And I considered him to be an Uncle Tom.... At that time, you didn't really listen to any of his music, you just had an impression of him, which came through the media, like most things. If I had met him ... I wouldn't have known who I was meeting.

KA What was the feeling on the street about Louis when you were growing up?

WM There was no feeling on the street about him. No one that I grew up with had ever heard of Louis Armstrong. The musicians knew who he was but they didn't listen to him.

KA Why was that?

WM Improper education and ignorance. The world knew who he was. Everybody else knew, just we didn't know. It's like what happens in America now. People don't really know somebody like Duke Ellington. Nobody really has heard his music. How many people have really heard Louis Armstrong play the trumpet—not that many people.... We don't have good education. Nobody really teaches us that we should care about it. So we don't care— there's a lot of other stuff to care about.

KA When did you discover Louis?

WM When I was about nineteen or twenty. My daddy sent me a tape of him. And for some reason I put the tape on and listened to it. I tried to learn one of the solos—"Jubilee."

KA And did you learn it?

WM I couldn't play it. I still probably can't play that solo. I mean, just the endurance of it … and the brilliance of it. But it sounds so natural and easy when he's playing, you don't realize what it is that he's playing. And if you try to learn it you realize it.

KA Which of Louis' recordings influenced your playing most strongly? Obviously that, "Jubilee."

WM All the Hot Five, Hot Seven, the stuff from the '30s, the '50s, I listen to all of it.

KA When you listen to Armstrong now, what do you take away from the music, not as a musician, but just as a person?

WM A depth of humanity of his playing. He's always telling you 'it's going to be all right'. Whatever those specific emotions that can be projected through music are, they're in his music. Joy. Sorrow. Things that there are no words for. His consciousness—which is a very high consciousness—comes through his sound.

KA Do you think that people, when they heard Louis, for instance in the movies that he was in, do you think that the jazz affected them or was it merely the name?

WM Well they had to be affected because everybody was imitating him. You have to realize that at one time he was the most popular musician in the world. All the musicians imitated him, so whether or not they heard *him* in the movies, they were going to hear something that sounded like him. The general person might not have known they were listening to Louis Armstrong, but in fact they were. He's the one who brought jazz to everybody. Whether they knew what it was, or… probably didn't know, it was what it was. Like if you look at a basketball game, do you know what Michael Jordan is doing? No, but you know who he is, and you know that everybody wants to play like him—that's like Louis Armstrong would be. Except more. He swept the world more. Even without the electronic media, he was a tremendous star. Bigger than anything.

KA So he revolutionized the music world.

WM And music in the entire world. Louis Armstrong could go on tour in Europe and they'd have a band in every city who knew his music. People loved him. I mean, he was Louis Armstrong.

KA In your book you wrote that one of the great lessons of jazz is that, as a musician you make room for someone else, help them sound good, then use a part of what they are playing to sound good yourself. Is finding that sort of conversation in jazz a good guideline for listening to the music? And for listening to Louis?

WM With Louis Armstrong it was a little different. Because everybody was trying to sound like him, he's in a unique position…. You don't want him to make room for anybody else. You want to hear *him* play. So that's a good guideline for jazz on certain songs, like the modern jazz that became more conversational. The early Louis Armstrong with King Oliver was more like that. He's playing with King Oliver, and he's listening, and he's playing….

KA What two or three of Louis' songs, or his recordings, would you recommend to somebody who wants to get to know him? What did you just play for me?

WM That was "I Got A Right to Sing the Blues" from 1931 or '32. Anything from the Hot Five or the Hot Seven. The "West End Blues" is the one that's the most famous. That's from the Hot Seven. "Azalea" from Louis Armstrong and Duke Ellington. "Azalea"— it's beautiful the way he plays that. Also … [sings a few notes] … "Tight Like This." "Cornet Chop Suey."

Hearing Louis *Armstrong for the first time around*

...he age of fourteen or fifteen was an incredible experience.

hello mister Armstrong

hearing Louis Armstrong for the first time around the age of fourteen or fifteen was an incredible experience. It was irresistible, a new idea that carried us far away, across the Atlantic—from our French family holiday in Fouras, Charente-Maritime, to New York, a city of towering myths. For us, Armstrong was just so American, and that's what attracted us, as kids to a childhood dream. I still remember the bold, shimmering, snapping happiness of a trumpet solo, transparent and sharp like Bohemian crystal. Armstrong was that exotic Negro king whose voice of sandpaper, mist, and cinnamon came straight out of the bayous of the South and the molasses and murk of the Eastern metropolises, from Montparnasse at the midnight hour and the cold moons of New York.

Louis in Everyday Day's a Holiday

ike a Douanier Rousseau who turned into a Picasso, Armstrong, grandson of a slave, invented a music of freedom and desire, always ready to raise the roof. Henri Guillemin, a man who also waxed eloquent about Victor Hugo, wrote me one day that "Armstrong is a big cat with a hoarse purr who juggles with the stars." How did this rough-and-ready hick of only 5 feet 4 inches get from pushing carts of coal in the streets of New Orleans to his role as sublime musician and fairground giant—innovative and black?

From town to town, in the velvet dusk of the highways, Armstrong traveled the length and breadth of the American imagination. "Armstrong's circus!" they said, all those earnest folks and bad journalists. A clown they called him, an Uncle Tom even, deaf and blind as they were not to see the very real, radiant dignity that shone in theatres and dance halls, in recording studios and on celluloid. For soon he was being employed (the word is apt) by Hollywood as a barman, faithful servant, or stableman. Amidst the goofy actors and streamlined starlets, Armstrong just shrugged it off, turning the situation to his advantage. "A clown? Why not, if that's the way you want me!" The films have faded now well, everything but the presence of this inspired joker whose rolling eyes bespeak a noble, impulsive soul. Take *A Song is Born*. The studio said to Howard Hawks: "Don't put the black and the white musicians too close to each other!" Hawks replied to the studio: "Get out of here! For me, Armstrong is music." Half a century later, the meteoric artist Jean-Michel Basquiat picked up the thread and put Louis Armstrong up there with his "black heroes" as the dedicatee of his *King of the Zulus*: Armstrong explosive in warm colors and vibrant undulations.

One morning, our "night passengers" hove up in Chicago, Scarface's town, where the bad boys called the shots behind the scenes and the big boys of jazz shot for the stars center-stage. After the gangster town (where Louis recorded his first sizzling 78s with the Hot Five in 1925), the next stop was New York, a town emerging from its Depression. Swing was in the air in the era of the New Deal.

Armstrong, craftsman of polished phrases, was clapped in the golden chains of entertainment. His name sizzled in letters of fire outside the palaces of the night: Louis Armstrong, the world's greatest trumpeter, at the Sunset Café. Everyone in the profession wanted to see him, hear him, touch him. "Louis was the hero of the hour," remembers Rex Stewart, a trumpeter with Duke Ellington. "I was crazy about him, like everyone else in town. I tried to walk like him, to talk like him. I waited outside his door for hours, just to see him passing by..." Another colleague, Jack Purvis, went so far as to name a record *Copyin' Louis*. No easy task!

Melody Maker.

meanwhile, the Old World was boiling with impatience, dancing to the crazy rhythm beat out by the "black phenomenon" in his Harlem smithy. In Paris, Jacques Becker collected his records and played them to his "boss," Jean Renoir. Fifty years before Woody Allen in Manhattan, the groupies of *l'art nègre*, Michel Leiris, Robert Desnos, Philippe Soupault, Marcel Duhamel, Alejo Carpentier, and Jean Cocteau, were all listening to "Cornet Chop Suey" and "Potato Head Blues." And then our illustrious passenger fetched up in Southampton.

In August 1934, Louis let the good times roll in Paris at the Brasserie Boudon, Cabane Cubaine, Villa d'Este, and Brick Top. In *L'Action Française*, the fascist Rebatet spit his franc's worth of venom: "Faux crude, a sham, and a ham." Another poison pen in *Je suis partout* picked up the baton: "This one's a real pure nigger, a primate straight from his tropical coconut tree." New Order, old stupidity.

In Marseille, between *Boudu sauvé des eaux* and *Toni*, Renoir caught every concert at the aptly named Palais de Cristal. Le Corbusier, *très chic*, went to hear "the black titan of the cry" in New York, where the cathedrals are white. The world was Armstrong's oyster. But later, when Official America, the State Department, tried

Following pages:
Louis and his wife Lucille in Egypt.

11

to transform the black pearl into an "ambassador of goodwill," the grit was still there. And the anger. "Things are so bad in the United States," he declared, "that the Blacks get the feeling they have no homeland. Eisenhower let them persecute my brothers. He can go to the devil."

africa, too, opened its arms. Satchmo went back to his roots, the savanna of his distant ancestors. This was no ordinary tour, but a sudden short-cut through time as the diaspora of yesterday's slaves pieced together the puzzle. In Accra, Ghana, the schoolkids greeted him with a resounding "Hello Mister Armstrong!" Negritude was a new idea. "Armstrong is the voice of the gorilla and the voice of the turtledove," wrote the poet and President of Senegal, Léopold Senghor.

Then, one day, the advancing years. Breath is short, the heart weak. Satchmo still sings, but seldom lifts his Selmer to his lips. He cuts roses from his garden in Corona, New York for Lucille, the former chorus girl. He shares his wisdom with local kids. And then sleep comes, the sleep of the just. They cover him with flowers. A concert of praises, the trumpets of immortal fame. Statues are raised, medals engraved, stamps issued. How could we ever forget this contemporary giant? "I'll never let the trumpet kill me," he liked to joke, "because I'll kill it first."

In his songs about the women of Saint Louis, "Ramona" and "Dolly," about dusk falling on the Old South, from the *Threepenny Opera*, or about "La Vie en rose," in those barnstorming trumpet lines, Satchmo is with us still. In a thousand-and-one solos distilled in a thousand-and-one nights, there is a blossom of dazzling beauty and a world of serene daring.

Balance and bravura. The story of A.

Michel Boujut

Louis and Lucille in their garden in Corona.

Louis Armstrong,
the illegitimate son
of William Armstrong
and Mary Albert
(Mayann), was born
on August 4, 1901
in James Alley,
New Orleans,
between Perdido
and Poydras streets.
All his life,
however,
it was thought
that he came
into the world
on July 4, 1900.
After all,
what could be
more fitting
for a great
twentieth-century
American
hero?

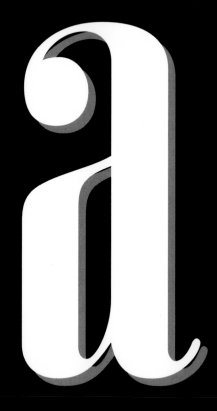

life

1901

AUGUST 4 According to a baptismal certificate written in Latin and found in the register of the Church of the Sacred Heart of Jesus Christ, Louis Armstrong, the illegitimate son of William Armstrong and Mary Albert (Mayann), is born in James Alley, between Perdido and Poydras streets, New Orleans. All his life, however, it was thought that he came into the world on July 4, 1900: Independence Day, and the first year of the new century to boot. ■

"James Alley.... is located in the crowded section of New Orleans known as Back o'Town.... In that one block between Gravier and Perdido streets more people were crowded than you ever saw in your life. There were churchpeople, gamblers, hustlers, cheap pimps, thieves, prostitutes and lots of children—and lots of women walking the streets for tricks.... Mayann told me that the night I was born there was a great big shooting scrape in James Alley and the two guys killed each other." When his parents separated, Louis was entrusted to Josephine Armstrong, his grandmother, "and when I grew up she was the one I called ma."

The house where Louis was born.

1904-1912

While his grandmother is busy taking in washing and ironing for the Whites, Louis divides his time between school, church, and the youth club, where he learns to sing. A short-lived attempt by his parents to get back together sees the birth of Beatrice Armstrong, who acquires the nickname Mama Lucy. ■ "I began to notice what was going on around me, especially in the honky-tonks in the neighborhood.... At the corner of the street where I lived was the famous Funky Butt Hall, where I first heard Buddy Bolden play. He was blowing up a storm.... Of course at the age of five I was not playing the trumpet, but there was something about the instrument that caught my ears. When I was in church and when I was 'second lining' — that is, following the brass bands in parades — I started to listen carefully to the different instruments, noticing the things they played and how they played them. That is how I learned to distinguish the differences between Buddy Bolden, King Oliver, and Bunk Johnson. No one had the fire and the endurance Joe had. No one in jazz has created as much music as he has. Almost everything important today came from him. Musicians from all over the world used to come to hear Joe Oliver..." ■ Louis goes to the Fisk School and learns to read. Some time later, he sells newspapers and does various odd jobs to help his mother, with whom he is now living again, at 1233 Perdido Street. But music is his passion and soon he forms a vocal trio, The Singing Fools, with two friends. He spends a lot of time with a Jewish family of rag pickers, the Karmofskys, whom he helps to gather scrap. Mrs. Karmofsky teaches him some old Russian songs. He buys a cornet and learns to play "Home Sweet Home." ■ Louis is spending more and more time in the honky-tonks. Bunk Johnson, who played at Dago Tony Tonk, remembers Little Louis (also known as Dippermouth and Gatemouth) slipping up onto the music stand: "He would fool around with my cornet every chance he got. I showed him just how to hold it and place it to his mouth.... Then I began showing him just how to start the blues." Louis Armstrong's reply: "Bunk didn't actually teach me anything. He didn't show me one thing!"

(*The Record Changer*, July-August 1950.)

An avenue in New Orleans at the turn of the century.

1913

JANUARY 1 On New Year's Day, Louis joins in the wild partying on the streets of New Orleans. To contribute to the general racket, he has armed himself with a big pistol, which he empties into the air. He is arrested and locked up at the Waif's Home, a "house of detention for colored boys" run by Captain Joseph Jones. ■ Peter Davis leads the home's brass band. Louis switches from the bass drum to the bugle and then, finally, to the cornet, which he practices assiduously. He soon establishes himself as the best brass player. ■ One day, Davis makes him leader: "I was in seventh heaven. Unless I was dreaming, my ambition had been realized.... Now at last I was not only a musician but a band leader!"

The Waif's Home Orchestra.

1914–1916

JUNE 16, 1914 Louis is free to go home. He is hired by various cabarets around town, as well as "for dances, picnics, funerals, and an occasional street parade on Sundays." ■ At the same time, he has a number of other jobs, either simultaneously or in quick succession: milkman, coalman, second-hand clothes seller, newspaper vendor. At the time, the most popular orchestra is led by trombonist Kid Ory. The cornet player, Joe Oliver, becomes Louis' master and protector, and finds him stand-in slots in a number of orchestras. "I often did errands for Stella Oliver, and Joe would give me lessons for my pay." ■ "I saw Louis playing in a band at a picnic. We didn't believe he could learn to play in that short time. I can still remember he was playing 'Maryland, My Maryland', and he sure was swingin' out that melody." (Zutty Singleton in *Hear Me Talkin' to Ya*)

1917

NOVEMBER 14 The US Navy has Storyville closed down in order to "safeguard the morale and morality of the troops." The bands are out of a job and many leave town.

*Louis
with his mother
and sister.*

1918

Louis gets a break. King Oliver has gone to Chicago to try his luck after the closing of Storyville, so Kid Ory offers Louis the vacant seat in his band, the Brown Skinned Babies. Louis is now a professional musician. ■ "After he joined me, Louis improved so fast it was amazing. He had a wonderful ear and a wonderful memory. All you had to do was hum or whistle a new tune to him and he'd know it right away." (Kid Ory in *Hear Me Talkin' to Ya*) Trombonist Preston Jackson: "We called him Dippermouth.... Louis played a horn like nobody had ever heard." ■ "I began to get real popular with the dance fans as well as the musicians. All the musicans came to hear us and they'd hire me to play in their bands on the nights I wasn't engaged by Kid Ory." ■ At the end of the year he marries Daisy Parker, a Creole prostitute he met at the Brick House, a working man's dance hall in Gretna, over the river, where he plays regularly on Saturday nights. Louis now takes it upon himself to bring up his cousin Flora's young son, Clarence Hatfield, whom he adopts.

*Riverboat
on the Mississippi.*

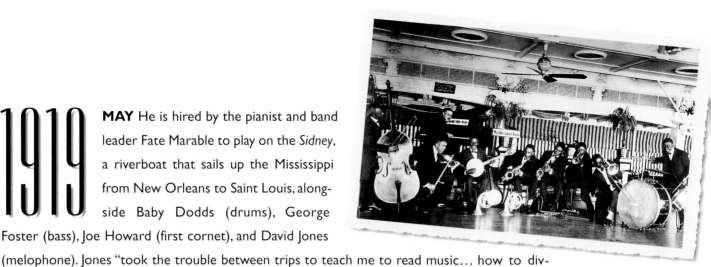

Fate Marable's Band.

1919

MAY He is hired by the pianist and band leader Fate Marable to play on the *Sidney*, a riverboat that sails up the Mississippi from New Orleans to Saint Louis, along-side Baby Dodds (drums), George Foster (bass), Joe Howard (first cornet), and David Jones (melophone). Jones "took the trouble between trips to teach me to read music… how to divide the notes." Louis could now play with remarkable confidence in all registers. ■ "At the Grand Central Hotel in St. Louis I was a very popular boy. Being the youngest fellow in Fate Marable's band, and single too, all the maids made a lot of fuss over me. I thought I was hot stuff when the gals argued over me…. I was too interested in my music to pay any attention to that sort of jive; to most of it anyway." ■ The young trombonist Jack Teagarden recalls: "At dawn, a friend and I were walking on the quayside at New Orleans. Suddenly I heard the distant sound of a trumpet. I couldn't see anything except a pleasure steamer sliding through the fog towards the port. Then the melody came through clearly. The boat was still quite far away, but close enough for me to make out a Black standing in the wind at the front, blowing one of the most beautiful notes I've ever heard. It was jazz…. I don't remember now if it was 'Tiger Rag' or 'Panama', but I do remember that it was Louis Armstrong, coming down from the skies like a god. I just stood there, listening and not moving until the boat dropped anchor. When the band came down, Fate Marable's band, I got to talking with the musicians and Marable introduced me to this unknown cornet player with the round, friendly face: Louis Armstrong."

1921

SEPTEMBER Fate Marable kicks Louis out after a brawl on the *Saint Paul*. "He looked so pathetic," remembers drummer Floyd Campbell, "sitting on his suitcase, waiting for the train that would take him back to New Orleans. He was crying his heart out and moaning 'What's going to happen to me?'" ■ **WINTER** In New Orleans, he works at the Orchard Cabaret, where his friend Zutty Singleton has set up a small band. He earns about twenty dollars a week. Then he moves on to Tom Anderson's The Real Thing in the company of Barney Bigard, Albert Nicholas, and Luis Russell, while becoming a permanent member of the Tuxedo Brass Band led by trumpeter Papa Celestin. He also takes part in street parades with the musicians of the Silver Leaf Band and Allen's Brass Band. ■ After four years of marriage and a long period of living apart, Daisy and Louis divorce.

1922

JULY Louis gets a telegram from King Oliver in Chicago offering him second trumpet in his Creole Jazz Band. "I arrived in Chicago about eleven o'clock the night of July 8th, 1922, I'll never forget it, at the Illinois Central Station.... I took a cab and went directly to the Gardens.... When I got inside and near the bandstand, King Oliver spied me. He immediately stopped the band to greet me, saying, 'Boy, where have you been? I've been waiting and waiting for you.'" The band features King Oliver (trumpet), Johnny Dodds (clarinet), Honore Dutrey (trombone), Baby Dodds (drums), Bill Johnson (bass), and Lilian Hardin (piano). "Those were some thrilling days of my life that I shall never forget. During my first night on the job, while things were going down in order, King and I stumbled

Louis and King Oliver.

upon a little something that no other two trumpeters together ever thought of. While the band was just swinging, the King would lean over to me, moving his valves on his trumpet, making notes, the notes that he was going to make when the break in the tune came. I'd listen, and at the same time I'd be figuring out my second to his lead. When the break would come, I'd have my part to blend right along with his. The crowd would go mad over it! King Oliver and I got so popular blending that jive together that pretty soon all the white musicians from downtown Chicago would all come there after work." (*Hear Me Talkin' to Ya*) ■ Muggsy Spanier: "I would go down to the South Side and listen hour after hour to those two great trumpeters, Joe King Oliver and Louis.... It got so that I knew every phrase and intonation they played, just from listening, so that, in spite of myself, I was doing the same things....You can imagine the thrill it was the first time they let me sit in with them and play....Gosh, I wish

I could describe the way those two used to play those pretty breaks! Nothing in the world was like it." (*Hear Me Talkin' to Ya*) ■ Tommy Brookins: "On that evening when he was sick, Oliver played as a member of the ensemble but let Louis solo and, believe me, Louis really played.... One can say that from that time on there was a question only of Louis. The school kids began to imitate the acts of 'Satchmo'. Hearing Louis after Oliver it seemed that Louis was more powerful."

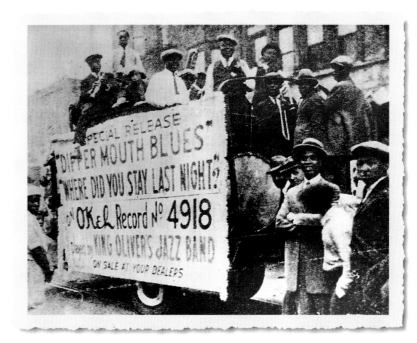

Parade for King Oliver's Jazz Band in 1923.

1923

MARCH The Creole Jazz Band cuts its first record for the Gennett Record Company in Chicago. King Oliver's band goes on tour in Illinois, Ohio, and Indiana. On March 31, in Richmond, the Starr Piano Company records ten sides using the acoustic horn system. They are released by Gennett. On "Chimes Blues" (April 6), Louis records his first solo—two choruses built on a phrase of King Oliver's which would later be used as the theme for the famous "In the Mood." Louis has such a powerful sound that the engineers have to stand him several yards behind the other musicians. The band returns to the Lincoln Gardens in Chicago. ■ **LATE DECEMBER** The band records three tracks for Paramount ("Riverside Blues," "Mabel's Dream," and "Southern Stomp"). They are seen by Hoagy Carmichael, who is with Bix Beiderbecke: "I dropped my cigarette and gulped my drink. Bix was on his feet, his eyes popping. For taking the first chorus was that second trumpet, Louis Armstrong. Louis was taking it fast.... Every note Louis hit was perfection."

Louis and the King Oliver Creole Jazz Band.

1924

FEBRUARY 5 Louis marries Lil Hardin. ■ On tour through May: Ohio, Wisconsin, Michigan, Pennsylvania. ■ Louis, who is already an excellent "reader," studies collections of cornet solos with Lil and takes a few lessons with a German teacher at Kimball Hall. ■ **JUNE** Tiring of his role as second cornet, and pushed by Lil's ambition, Louis leaves Oliver's band for Ollie Powers's group at Dreamland. In a letter to his friend Bunk Johnson, Oliver comments on the young Louis: "Man, he really can play now. You should see how easily he pulls out those high Fs and Gs." ■ **SEPTEMBER** The bandleader Fletcher Henderson invites Louis to come and join him at the Roseland Ballroom in New York. Louis tells everyone that this is his big chance. "Fletcher led the first black big band, the one that showed all the others the way. And here I was about to join the greatest band in town." ■ **OCTOBER 13** Louis arrives in New York. Over the coming months he becomes the toast of Harlem. He staggers fellow musicians with his inventive prowess. Trumpeter Rex Stewart: "Then Louis Armstrong hit town! I went mad with the rest of the town. I

Louis with the Fletcher Henderson Orchestra.

tried to walk like him, talk like him, eat like him, sleep like him. I even bought a pair of big policeman shoes like he used to wear and stood outside his apartment waiting for him to come out so I could look at him. Finally, I got to shake hands." Duke Ellington: "The guys had never heard anything just like it. There weren't the words coined for describing that kick. And Louis was no exception, he carried his horn round just like everybody else, and sat in and played anywhere he happened to drop in. Everyone on the street was talking about the guy." Coleman Hawkins: "An orgy of music! Fletcher's musicians played like demons. The high point was when Louis Armstrong reeled off a dozen choruses on 'Shanghai Shuffle'. When the piece was over, a dancer bore Louis in triumph. And there I was, silent, slack-jawed, almost ashamed, wondering if I would ever be capable of having just a tiny bit of Louis' greatness." Among the forty-odd sides he cuts with the Fletcher Henderson band, "The Meanest Kind of Blues," "Mandy Make Up Your Mind," "One of These Days," "Money Blues," and most of all, "Sugar Foot Stomp," cause a sensation thanks to Louis' superb solos. Louis also makes his debut as a singer.

An avenue in Harlem,
New York City, at the turn of the century.

1925

Regularly invited to accompany blues singers including Maggie Jones, Trixie Smith, and Ma Rainey, Louis cuts many records as a sideman. The most important are those he makes with Bessie Smith: *Saint Louis Blues, Reckless Blues, Cold in Hand Blues* (January 24). He also makes a few songs with studio bands, notably the Clarence Williams group with Sidney Bechet on soprano saxophone. Louis' final chorus makes "Everybody Loves My Baby" such a hit that the pressings sell out as soon as they hit the shops. Musicians soon know the chorus by heart. During his stint at the Roseland, through May 31, Louis also plays at many private parties. ■ **SUMMER** On tour: Connecticut, Maine, Maryland, Massachusetts, and Pennsylvania. ■ **NOVEMBER** He leaves Fletcher Henderson and returns to Chicago to play in the band led by his wife at the Dreamland Cafe. Louis is making seventy-five dollars a week. The black newspaper, *The Chicago Defender,* announces that Lil's Dreamland Syncopators will be featuring "the world's greatest jazz cornet player." Louis forms a studio band for OKeh. This is the first of the celebrated series of recordings by Louis Armstrong's Hot Five: Johnny Dodds (clarinet), Kid Ory (trombone), John St. Cyr (banjo), and Lil Armstrong (piano). The first (acoustic) recording session is held in the OKeh studios on November 12: "Gut Bucket Blues," "My Heart," "Yes I'm In The Barrel." "I don't know who got the idea for the Hot Five records. It may have been Richard M. Jones, who worked for the OKeh company at the time…. I think one reason those records came out so well was that the OKeh people left us alone…. Another reason was that we all knew each other's musical styles so well from years

Louis Armstrong and his Hot Five in 1925

of working together. And then, of course, there was Louis, you can't go wrong with Louis." (Kid Ory in *Hear Me Talkin' to Ya*) A month after his debut at Dreamland, Louis is hired by Erskine Tate's band at the Vendome Theatre. He switches from cornet to trumpet. "[Fats Waller] and I used to play in the Symphony Orchestra in Chicago in 1925. It was at the Vendome Theatre, a motion picture house. That was in the days of silent films….We used to play for the films, and during the intermission, we would play a big Overture and a Red Hot Number afterwards. And folks, I'm telling you, we used to really romp." His solo rendering of "Cavalleria Rusticana" becomes a specialty. Bill Coleman: "When Louis cut his first Hot Five, I was the first person in Cincinnati to buy it. And every week I went back to the shop to see if the new Armstrongs had come in. I started imitating his solos, note by note, the ones in 'Mandy Make Up Your Mind' and 'Money Blues'."

1926

FEBRUARY 26 New session: "Heebie Jeebies," "Muskrat Ramble," "Cornet Chop Suey." "When we recorded 'Heebie Jeebies'," recalls John St. Cyr, "the sound man insisted that we have a vocal. So Louis went and sat down in a corner and began hastily jotting down some words. We did one or two trial takes which went like clockwork, but when we were actually recording, Louis dropped the sheet he'd written the lyrics on, and since he didn't want to spoil the polish, scatted the rest of the vocal. The result was a record that influenced countless other singers." (*Bulletin du Hot Club de France,* no. 160). ■ **MARCH–APRIL** Louis leaves Dreamland to join the Carroll Dickerson orchestra at the Sunset Cafe, but continues to play at the Vendome. For the first time, his name is up in lights at the front of the Sunset as "the world's greatest trumpet player." "After the theater I'd go over to the Sunset... and

Louis Armstrong and his Stompers at the Sunset Cafe.

swing there with them until the wee hours of the morning. 'Twas great, I'll tell you. In that band there were Earl Hines, Darnell Howard, Tubby Hall, Honore Dutrey, and Boyd Atkins.... The Sunset had Charleston

contests on Friday night, and you couldn't get a place unless you got there early.... We had a finale that just wouldn't quit.... Percy Venable, the producer of the show, staged a finale with four of us band boys closing the show doing the Charleston. That was really something." ■ **JUNE 12** The Hot Five make their one and only public appearance, during a show at the Chicago Coliseum with all the town's great jazzmen. In a special edition, the *Chicago Defender* speaks of "Louis Armstrong, the miracle with steel lips." ■ The Hot Five continue their recordings: "King of the Zulus," "Lonesome Blues," "Jazz Lips," "Skid-da-de-dat," "Sunset Cafe," "Big Butter and Egg Man." ■ **AUGUST** Louis takes three weeks' vacation with Lil in Idlewild, Michigan. ■ **WINTER** Ray Ventura: "When I found out that the boat from America was coming into Le Havre, I played hooky and rushed to the shop in the Rue des Italiens to buy all the new records by Louis Armstrong, who was my favorite."

1927

At the beginning of the year, the Dickerson Orchestra leaves the Sunset Cafe and Louis fills the slot with a small band, L.A. and His Stompers, featuring Earl Hines on piano and Tubby Hall on drums. Benny Goodman, Jess Stacy, Bix Beiderbecke, the Dorsey Brothers, and many other white musicians flock to hear them. "Those were the days when all the musicians used to go down the South Side several times a week just to hear Louis and Earl. It was a ritual: every Friday after work we piled into the Sunset." (Freddy Goodman) He plays with Erskine Tate at the Vendome through to April, then to December at the Metropolitan Theater with Clarence Jones. ■ **MAY** The Hot Five becomes the Hot Seven with the addition of Peter Briggs on the tuba and Baby Dodds on drums. John Thomas replaces Kid Ory. Recordings: "Willie the Weeper," "Wild Man Blues," "Potato Head Blues," "Melancholy Blues," "Weary Blues," "Twelfth Street Rag," "Gully Low Blues." Ralph Glaser, owner

Louis Armstrong and the Luis Russel Orchestra.

of the Sunset, and Louis' future manager: "All of them records were made from about six to nine in the mornings.... Louis would leave the club at three, four, five a.m." ■ The actress Tallulah Bankhead plays the recording of "Potato Head Blues" every night on stage in *Private Lives*, the play that she performs for three consecutive years on Broadway. The Melrose Bros. Music Company in Chicago publishes two sets of scores: *Louis Armstrong's 50 Hot Choruses for Cornet* and *Louis Armstrong's 125 Jazz Breaks for Cornet*. ■ **JULY** Two-week date at the Blackhawk. ■ **SEPTEMBER** Back to the Hot

Five formula: "Put'em Down Blues," "Ory's Creole Trombone," "The Last Time," "Struttin' With Some Barbecue," "I'm Not Rough," "Hotter Than That," "Savoy Blues." These records make Louis' name all over America. ■ **NOVEMBER** Louis, Earl Hines, and Zutty Singleton open their own dance room, Warwick Hall. It closes after only a few weeks.

1928

MARCH–APRIL Louis joins Carroll Dickerson at the Savoy Ballroom, a newly opened establishment in Harlem, where he is a roaring success. The posters advertise "Special attraction. The great Louis Armstrong in person!" Drummer George Wettling: "When Louis started blowing the introduction to 'West End Blues' (man was it mellifluous), everybody in the ballroom started screaming and whistling, and then Louis lowered the boom and everybody got real groovy when he went into the first strains of 'West End'." (*Hear Me Talkin' to Ya*) The trumpet player Wingy Manone remembers seeing Louis "literally carried in triumph to the stage." ■ **MAY** Plays occasionally as a soloist outside Chicago, notably for two days in the band led by drummer Floyd Campbell on the SS *St. Paul* in Saint Louis for a hundred dollars a day. Crowds pour in to see an exceptional attraction: "Louis Armstrong vs Al Trent in a Battle of the Bands." ■ **JUNE, JULY, AND DECEMBER**

Second set of sessions by the Louis Armstrong Hot Seven, this time with Earl Hines (piano), Zutty Singleton (drums), Mancy Cara (banjo), Fred Robinson (trombone), Jimmy Strong (clarinet and alto saxophone), and Don Redman (alto saxophone). Result—a handful of masterpieces: "West End Blues," "Fireworks," "Basin Street Blues," "Saint James Infirmary," "No One Else But You," "Tight Like This." When, during a short stay in Chicago, Fletcher Henderson tries to get Louis to join his band, the Savoy has to pay him a cachet of two hundred dollars a night to make him stay on. ■ Earl Hines: "When I came up to Chicago I was amazed to find a trumpeter like Louis who was playing everything that I was trying to do on the piano. So, there were the two of us expressing the same spirit, one on the trumpet, the other on the piano. You can imagine how we enjoyed playing together. And listening to what the other was doing… Like me, Louis was a carefree type. We were always hanging around together and getting into all sorts of adventures." In the words of Truman Capote, who tells of meeting him on a Mississippi pleasure steamer, Louis is now "a hard-plump and belligerently happy brown Buddha."

1929

JANUARY–MAY Louis and Carroll Dickerson are working regularly at the Savoy Ballroom, but also from time to time at the Graystone Ballroom, in Detroit (January and March), and in Saint Louis (February). ■ **MARCH** In New York, Louis plays for two hours with the Luis Russell Orchestra: J. C. Higginbotham (trombone), Albert Nicholas (clarinet), Charlie Holmes (alto saxophone), Teddy Hill (tenor saxophone), Luis Russell (piano), Eddie Condon (banjo), Lonnie Johnson (guitar), Pops Foster (bass), Paul Barbarin (drums). With them he records "I Can't Give You Anything But Love" and "Mahogany Hall Stomp." ■ In Chicago he works with Dickerson again and plays with Dave Peyton's band at the Regal Theater (April 28–May 4). ■ **MAY** Plays at the Paradise Ballrooom, Cincinnati, on May 7. Then back in New York. ■ "My manager and agent sent for me to come to New York alone, to join that big show which was in rehearsal at that time called *Great Day*. Instead of going alone, I took the whole Carroll Dickerson band with me. We were so attached, we just wouldn't part from each other.... We had about four old dilapidated cars among us. We just piled in them and went on to New York. On our way we went sightseeing, stopping in a lot of towns where they'd been listening to us over the radio from the Savoy in Chicago. They treated us royally.... Half our cars didn't reach the 'Apple' (New York). They burned out before they reached halfway there. Of course my agent bawled me out, but I told him 'Just the same, my boys are here in New York, so find something for us to do.'" ■ In Philadelphia he rehearses with Fletcher Henderson's orchestra for the Vincent Youmans show *Great Day*. ■ **JUNE** Back to New York to direct Dickerson's band at the Savoy in Harlem (June 1 and 2). ■ Four month booking at Connie's Inn to accompany the *Hot Chocolate* review with the Leroy Smith band. This is when he first performs Fats Waller's song "Ain't Misbehavin'." At the premiere, all the musicians in the pit stand up to add their applause to that of the audience at the end of the show. Records "Ain't Misbehavin'," "Black and Blue," "Some of These Days." ■ **JULY** A banquet is organized in Louis' honor and he is given a gold watch ("To Louis Armstrong, the world's greatest cornetist, from the musicians of New York.") *Hot Chocolate* continues for 219 performances on Broadway, up to the end of the year. ■ **FALL–WINTER** Louis performs with the Luis Russell orchestra and as a "solo attraction" at the Lafayette and Rockland Palace in New York, then at the Standard Theater in Philadelphia. ■ In *Really the Blues* Mezz Mezzrow describes his popularity. "Louis always held a handkerchief in his hand because he perspired so much, onstage and off, and that started a real fad—before long, all the kids on The Avenue were running up to him with white handkerchiefs in their hands too, to show how much they loved him. Louis always stood with his hands clasped in front of him, in a kind of easy slouch. Pretty soon all the kids were hanging around The Corner with their hands locked in front of them, one foot in front of the other [...] All the raggedy kids, especially those who became vipers, were so inspired with self-respect after digging how neat and natty Louis was, they started to dress up real good." ■ **DECEMBER** Records with the Luis Russell orchestra: "Saint Louis Blues," "Dallas Blues," "I Ain't Got Nobody," "Rockin' Chair,"

"Song of the Island," "Bessie Couldn't Help It," "Blue Turning Grey Over You." Jack Purvis records an Armstrong pastiche entitled *Copyin' Louis*, and one night Jabbo Smith borrows Louis' trumpet and plays his lines in "West End Blues." Writing about Louis' latest recordings in *La Revue du Jazz,* the French trumpeter Philippe Brun notes: "This Black is incredibly bold. Nothing is too hot for him. He makes light work of every difficulty, his technique is so proficient. Armstrong is colored jazz in all its plenitude."

An avenue in Harlem, New York City in the '30s.

1930

FEBRUARY Starts a two-month booking at the Coconut Grove in New York, backed by the Mills Blue Rhythm Band, with which he cuts a few records and plays dates in Detroit, Baltimore, Philadelphia (April), Pittsburgh, and Chicago (May), then returns to New York. Johnny Collins, a notorious crook, becomes Louis' manager. ■ **APRIL 5** Recording of "Dear Old Southland," a trumpet solo accompanied by Buck Washington on piano. ■ **JULY** Leaves for California. "Most of the shows and night clubs," recalls saxophonist George James, "were controlled by the underworld. When he was in the *Hot Chocolate* show, he signed with a bigwig who directed the Cotton Club. Louis always found it hard to say no. Anyway, he soon realized that he'd got himself into a real mess, caught between rival gangs, and he decided to get as far from New York as he could." ■ In Culver City, a suburb of Los Angeles, he performs at Frank Sebastian's Cotton Club with a band conducted at first by Leon Elkins and then by the saxophonist Les Hite, and including the vibraphonist and drummer Lionel Hampton and the trombonist Lawrence Brown. "The nights we spent playing with him were marvelous," declares Brown. "Each time we were right on the edge of our seats, waiting breathlessly for the next phrase, as captived and certainly more excited than the audience itself." ■ Among the stars of the silver screen who come to see the "phenomenon of the trumpet" are Jean Harlow, Carole Lombard, Marlene Dietrich, Douglas Fairbanks, James Cagney, Humphrey Bogart, and the Marx Brothers. Bing Crosby recalls, "I went there to listen to him all the time. When Louis plays, he soars. When he sings, he sparkles." Louis waxes a few songs,

including "I'm a Ding Dong Daddy." Lionel Hampton remembers: "I played drums in his band and I was crazy about him. I wanted to play everything Louis played. Since I couldn't reproduce on the drums what he was doing on the trumpet, I started playing vibraphone. Louis was wonderful with me. When I tried to play vibraphone in 'Memories

"AMERICA'S LEADING COLORED THEATRE"

LAFAYETTE
7TH AVE — 132 ST.

NOW PLAYING (UP TO SUNDAY, JUNE 30, INC.)

The World's Greatest Cornetist

LOUIS ARMSTRONG

AND HIS FAMOUS CHICAGO BAND

In Addison Carey's Revue

"MOVE ALONG"

With (UKELELE) BOB WILLIAMS, GALLIE DE GASTON, JOE BYRD, HONEY BROWN
And Other Musical Comedy Favorites

— Also The Photoplay Hit —

REGINALD DENNY in "CLEAR THE DECKS"

Next Week—Beginning Monday, July 1

AL JOLSON in "THE SINGING FOOL"

Also the Musical Riot—"SAM FROM RAM"
With Lillian Brown and Emmett Anthony

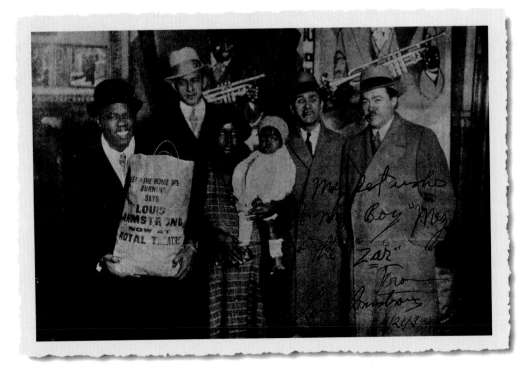

Distribution of charcoal (right : manager Johnny Collins).

of You', the guy who was supervising the session didn't want to let me take the introduction. But Louis said: 'Come on, let the kid play!'" (*Bulletin du Hot Club de France*, 1949). Aside from "Memories of You," Louis records "Sweethearts on Parade," "Shine," and "Confessin'." "I was walking in the street in Los Angeles when I heard a record that Louis had just made," recalls Buck Clayton, "and I stopped to listen. The playing was so beautiful I was incapable of moving on. I loved that record for its beauty." ■ Louis makes his film debut in *Flame* by Victor Halperin. He is arrested at the Cotton Club by the drugs squad and he and drummer Vic Berton are charged with "possession of marijuana in the form of cigarettes." The incident causes a big stir. The sentence, six months of prison and a thousand-dollar fine, is suspended after a few days. ■ **NOVEMBER 21** Louis gives out a thousand bags of coal to Blacks in the poor districts of Baltimore, Maryland. This charitable action is orchestrated by his manager, Johnny Collins. ■ Louis and Lil separate.

1931

SPRING At the Showboat in Chicago Louis becomes the leader of a new band formed for him by the trumpeter Zilner Randolph, his musical director. They record "When It's Sleepy Time Down South," "You Rascal You," "Lazy River." "In Chicago," Louis later recalled, "whenever you looked around you felt there was a gun pointing right at you."

Louis and Captain Jones.

Dinner at the Zulu's Club in New Orleans.

Everywhere he goes his bodyguard goes with him. Mid-May, he tours Illinois, Kentucky, Ohio, and Virginia. A week in Detroit, then Milwaukee and Minneapolis. ■ **JUNE** Returns to New Orleans and is given a triumphant reception by his fellow citizens. He visits the Waif's Home and meets the old director, Captain Jones. He gives his name to a local baseball team. He plays at the Suburban Gardens for three months, for a whites-only audience. At the first concert to be broadcast over the radio, a white presenter refuses to announce "that nigger." ■ **FALL–WINTER** On tour: Dallas, Oklahoma City, Houston, Memphis, Saint Louis, Columbus, Cincinnati, Cleveland, Philadelphia, Baltimore. In Memphis, the band spends a night in jail. "When the bus came into town," remembers one of the musicians, "they looked at us with staring eyes. Can you imagine it, black men all nattily dressed! And then there was Louis sitting out front, talking with a white woman, the wife of our manager Johnny Collins." Once released, Louis takes part in a radio program: "Ladies and gentlemen, my name is Louis Satchmo Armstrong. The boys and I are going to dedicate our first piece to the Officer of the Peace: 'I'll Be Glad When You're Dead, You Rascal You'." ■ He sees out the year at the Lincoln Theater in Philadelphia.

Louis and his orchestra at the Suburban Gardens.

34

1932

JANUARY Dates in New Haven, Jersey City, Boston, and New York. Back to Chicago in March. The band splits up. ■ **APRIL** Louis stays in California, where he plays at Sebastian's Cotton Club. In *Rhapsody in Black and Blue,* a short film by Aubrey Scotto, Louis plays the "Negro King" and his band are all dressed in leopard skins. In *You Rascal You*, the Paramount film by Max Fleischer, he sings alongside the cartoon vamp Betty Boop. ■ **JULY** Sails from New York with Alpha Smith, his new companion, on board the SS *Majestic*. Upon his arrival in England (July 14), he is the guest of honor of the press. He does two weeks at the London Palladium backed by a group of black musicians recruited in Paris, including Peter DuCongé. The Belgian poet Robert Goffin is in the audience: "Monday at the Palladium it was fantastic. I have never known such emotion. The place was shaken like a steamship in stormy weather." Reporting the performance by "the colored phenomenon," *Melody Maker* prints: "While he sings, he holds a handkerchief in his hand and wipes his face…. He is, in short, a unique phenomenon, an electric personality, the finest America has ever sent us." Louis plays with English musicians at the Glasgow Empire, the Holborn Empire, and the Trocadero. ■ **OCTOBER** Louis and Alpha arrive in Paris, where they stay at the Grand Hôtel, Rue Scribe. He plays at the Brick Top, Pigalle, and meets the young critic Hugues Panassié. Johnny Collins's financial demands are so exorbitant that no contracts are signed and Louis leaves Paris without getting to perform. ■ **NOVEMBER 19** Back to New York. That very evening, he plays at Connie's Inn, where he is greeted by a standing ovation. He is booked through December 2 at the Lafayette Theater in a new version of *Hot Chocolate*, accompanied by drummer Chick Webb and his band. The young Joseph Losey, a friend of the critic John Hammond, comes to hear him several times with the novelist Vicky Baum, the actor Charles Laughton, and the Soviet filmmaker Sergei Eisenstein. ■ Although his lips are causing him pain, he records for *Victor* "That's My Home," "Hobo You Can't Ride This Train," and, with Chick Webb, plays at Philadelphia's Pearl Theater (December 3–10) and Lincoln Theater (December 17–24), and at the Howard Theater in Washington, D.C.

Louis in Rhapsody in Black and Blue.

Louis and his baseball team.

1933

JANUARY After Pittsburgh (January 14), Louis is in Chicago, where Zilner Randolph has formed a new band for him featuring Budd Johnson (tenor), Keg Johnson (trombone), and Teddy Wilson (piano). Concerts in Louisville, Indianapolis, Omaha, and Philadelphia. His lips are still hurting and this can be heard in his playing. ■ **MARCH 31** In London *The Daily Express* announces the death of the "trumpet player with lips of steel."

Melody Maker issues a correction (April 4), but the news is repeated around the world. ■ **JULY** Louis sets sail on the *Homeric* with Alpha for a European tour starting in London (Holborn Empire, August 5). He breaks with his manager, Johnny Collins, who is an incompetent and dishonest "slave driver." Collins's place is taken by the conductor and concert organizer Jack Hylton, who finds Louis some extra dates in England and also Scandinavia, where he is given a hero's welcome. In Denmark, he takes a role in *Kophenhagen Kalundborg,* a movie vaudeville made up of various musical numbers. The tour travels on to Holland, then back to England.

Louis in Paris where he lives in 1934.

Louis in Lausanne (Switzerland), December 1934.

1934

APRIL For a concert organized by *Melody Maker,* Jack Hylton tries to get Louis together with Coleman Hawkins, the tenor saxophonist from the Fletcher Henderson band, which has just arrived in London. Louis pulls out at the last minute. ■ **AUGUST** In Paris, he lives for a while in Bougival, then moves into furnished accommodations on the Rue de la Tour d'Auvergne. Among his new friends are the critics Hugues Panassié and Charles Delaunay, who run the Hot Club de France. Louis meets the French musicians Django Reinhardt, Stéphane Grappelli, and Alix Combelle. ■ **OCTOBER** Signs a contract with Jacques Canetti. Peter DuCongé puts together a band of West Indians and American Blacks based in Paris. They cut six sides under the supervision of Jacques Canetti, including "On the Sunny Side of the Street" (I and II), "Super Tiger Rag," and "The Saint Louis Blues." ■ **NOVEMBER–DECEMBER** Two concerts at the Salle Pleyel (November 9 and 10). Makes a forty-minute radio appearance on *Le Poste Parisien:* "Not only does Louis Armstrong play the trumpet like

Louis and Alpha Smith.

a god, but he also sings. His voice, which sounded harmonious on record, is, on its own, weak and somewhat rough, more suited to comic effects than to charm." (*L'Intransigeant,* November 18). ■ Tours Belgium (November 13–25: Brussels, Antwerp, Liège, Ghent), the Netherlands (the Doelezaal, Rotterdam), Switzerland (Théâtre Lumen and Hôtel Palace, Lausanne; Grosser Kasinosaal, Bern; Kursaal, Montreux; Zurich). In France, he plays in Strasbourg, Dijon, Lyon, Marseille (where movie director Jean Renoir is in the audience), and Montpellier. The tour is planned to go on to North Africa and Egypt, but the state of Louis' lips forces him to quit after two concerts in Turin. He returns to Paris.

Louis and Arita Day at Brussels station, 1934.

1935

JANUARY Breaking his contract, he boards the SS *Champlain* at Le Havre (January 24). He is involved in a controversy with Jacques Canetti, which is reported in the second issue of *Jazz-Hot*. At the Local 208 in Chicago, the American Federation of Musicians holds a ball in honor of his return. Louis does not play his trumpet again until the summer. On February 14 he sings with the Duke Ellington Orchestra. A reception is given at Tony's Tavern in honor of the two musicians. Joe Glaser becomes his new manager (Associated Booking Corporation). He negotiates a contract with the new firm Decca for the next recordings. ■ **JULY** Louis forms a band with fifteen musicians and goes on tour through the Midwest and the southern states, down to New Orleans. "In those days it was real hell for a black man to play down in the South. When you were touring it was impossible to find a decent place to eat, sleep or just go to the toilet." ■ **SEPTEMBER** The tour terminates at the Apollo Theater in New York. He has a three-year contract with the Luis Russell orchestra. Their concerts at Connie's Inn (from October 29) are broadcast four times a week. *Esquire* and *Vanity Fair* both publish Armstrong features.

Louis in Lausanne, 1934.

1936

Publication in New York of *Swing That Music* (Longman), Louis' ghost-written memoirs. Among his many recordings are "Lying to Myself," "Ev'n Tide" (with his big band), and "Dippermouth Blues" (with Jimmy Dorsey). ■ **MARCH** Does a week at the Apollo Theater, then at the Metropolitan, Boston. His fee is $8,000 a week. On tour: Pittsburgh (May), Detroit (June), Saint Louis and Chicago (July), Kansas City (August). ■ **AUGUST** Makes *Pennies from Heaven* (Columbia), by Norman McLeod, with Bing Crosby, in which he plays "Skeleton in the Closet" with a small band featuring Lionel Hampton on drums. Embarks on a tour of one-nighters with the Luis Russell orchestra: Texas, Philadelphia, Virginia (September); Chicago, Washington, D.C., Savannah (October); Chicago again, New York, Saint Louis (November, at which time he also visits Fate Marable on the *Saint Paul*); Youngstown, and Akron (December). Christmas holidays in Chicago. ■ **DECEMBER** In France, *Jazz-Hot* awards "Old Man Mose" its Grand Prix for best recording.

*Party in honor
of Duke Ellington and Louis Armstrong
at Tony's Tavern, Chicago, 1936.*

PARTY IN HONOR OF
DUKE ELLINGTON AND LOUIS ARMSTRONG
AT TONY'S TAVERN - 51 W 31ST STREET
FEB. 14 1935 - CHICAGO - ILL.

Louis and the Luis Russell orchestra.

1937

JANUARY Louis spends a few days at the Provident Hospital in Chicago for a minor throat operation. Concerts in Omaha, Boston (February); Massachusetts, Pennsylvania (March); and New York (April). Series of radio broadcasts sponsored by Fleischmann's Yeast. Dates at the Regal Theater in Chicago, and the Apollo in New York (May); in Connecticut (June); Pittsburgh and Washington (July); Boston and the Southern States (September); and California (November and December). ■ Makes appearances in several Hollywood films: *Artists and Models* by Raoul Walsh, with Jack Benny (Paramount); *Doctor Rhythm* by Frank Tuttle, with Bing Crosby (Paramount), in which he performs "The Trumpet Player's Lament"; and *Everyday's a Holiday* by Edward Sutherland, with Mae West (Paramount), in which he leads the vamp's electoral parade playing "Jubilee." ■ Recordings: "Darling Nelly Grey," "Yours and Mine," "She's the Daugher of a Planter from Havana," "When the Saints," "Confessin'."

Louis in **Goin' Places.**

1938

JANUARY The end of a month-long slot at the Cotton Club, Culver City. At the Grand Terrace, Chicago, January 28–March 9. ■ **APRIL 10** Death of King Oliver in Savannah, Georgia. "We had his body brought over to New York. All the musicians of New York were there to see the man who gave us all a start for the last time. I am desperate at the idea that he has left this earth." (*Jazz-Hot*, April–May 1938). ■ **JUNE–AUGUST** Plays in Indianapolis, Pittsburgh, New York, Cincinnati. Six-week tour in the South. ■ **SEPTEMBER** Louis performs "Jeepers Creepers" in Ray Enright's film *Goin' Places,* with Dick Powell and Maxine Sullivan (Warner Bros.). He plays the role of a stable boy and trumpeter whose instrument is the only thing that can get a reaction from his horse(!). Rejoins the band for the rest of the tour: Mississippi, Louisiana, Alabama, and Georgia. ■ **OCTOBER** Louis marries Alpha Smith in Houston, Texas (they have been living together since 1931). Dates in New Orleans, Memphis, and Kansas City, then Detroit, Chicago, and New York. ■ **DECEMBER** After a concert at the Paramount Theater, Louis jams with Tommy Dorsey, Bud Freeman, Pops Foster, Eddie Condon, Henry "Red" Allen, and George Wettling. ■ He sings in Paul Whiteman's band at the Christmas concert at Carnegie Hall. He makes his only recordings with the pianist Fats Waller during a radio broadcast with DJ Martin Bloch (December 12).

*Louis and Maxine Sullivan
in* Swing in the Dream, *1939.*

1939

JANUARY Plays at the Strand Theater, New York, then tours theaters and ballrooms in Baltimore, Kansas City, Hartford, Buffalo, Olcott, Chicago, Lovejoy, Indianapolis, Atlanta, Madison, Miami, Columbia, Owensburg, Dayton, and Cleveland. ■ **OCTOBER 19** He plays at the Golden Gate Ballroom and the Cotton Club in New York. "At a referendum organized by *Down Beat* the trophy was awarded to Harry James. He simply refused it and said: 'Take that back and give it to Louis Armstrong.'" (Philly Jo Jones) ■ **NOVEMBER** Louis plays the role of Bottom in the jazz version of *A Midsummer Night's Dream* on Broadway, playing opposite Maxine Sullivan's Titania, Queen of the Night. This "theatrical extravaganza" is panned by the critics and lasts only eleven days.

Jazz version of **A Midsummer Night's Dream.**

1940

The engagement at the Cotton Club ends April 5. ■ **MAY 27** For Decca, he records "Perdido," "Street Blues," "2/19 Blues," "Down in Honky Tonk Town," and "Cool Cart Blues," with Sidney Bechet. ■ Concerts at the State Lake, Chicago (June) and the Apollo and Paramount in New York, followed by dates in Alabama, Georgia, South Carolina, Iowa (August), Chicago (September), California (October), Mississippi and Florida (November–December). ■ The tenor saxophonist Joe Garland becomes his musical director. ■ Makes some scopitones for Panoram: "Shine," "When It's Sleepy Time Down South," "Swingin' or Nothing," "I'll Be Glad When You're Dead, You Rascal You."

1941

JUNE Continues his coast-to-coast touring. ■ Dates in Toronto. Records "Hey Lawdy Mama," and "Now Do You Call That a Buddy" with members of his band. ■ **JULY** Orson Welles plans to film a life of Louis Armstrong under the title *Jazz Story,* scripted by Elliot Paul, with Armstrong playing himself.

*Sidney Bechet,
Clarence Williams,
and Louis.*

*Following pages:
Louis in Artists
and Models.*

1942

MARCH–APRIL Booked at the Casa Mañana, Culver City, California. ■ **AUGUST** Makes *Cabin in the Sky* with Vincente Minnelli, in which Louis, a "trumpeter from hell," appears with two little horns on his head. ■ The American Federation of Musicians orders an all-out strike. The unionized artists desert the studios. The record industry is paralyzed for two years. ■ **OCTOBER 2** His divorce with Alpha is officially declared. On tour, on October 7, he weds the young chorus girl Lucille Wilson in Saint Louis, Missouri. "Something tells me that this time it's serious," says Louis. "I fell in love with her because of the color of her skin. When she was dancing at the Cotton Club she was the darkest in the troupe." ■ Buys a house in Corona, New York.

Lionel Hampton, Arnett Cobb, Louis, and Red Allen.

1943

MARCH End of his tour, and back to New York city. ■ Louis takes part in a three-way radio jam session with Benny Goodman and Duke Ellington. ■ He forms a new big band, with Teddy McRae as musical director. ■ Writes to Zutty Singleton: "My lips are all messed up. I want to cancel some concerts but in this business you have to be dead to cancel!"

1944

JANUARY 18 For the *Esquire* awards ceremony at the Metropolitan Opera House, Louis, voted "musician of the year," performs with the leading musicians from the other categories: Coleman Hawkins, Jack Teagarden, Barney Bigard, Art Tatum, Al Casey, Oscar Pettiford, Lionel Hampton, Red Norvo, Sidney Catlett, Roy Eldridge, and Billie Holliday. The songs recorded at this concert, "Flying on a V-Disc," "Basin Street Blues," "Back o' Town Blues," are issued on a V-disc (Victory discs for American soldiers at the front). ■ Films: *Atlantic City* by Ray McCarey, *Hollywood Canteen* by Delmer Davis, *Jam Session* by Charles T. Barton, in which he plays his own compositions, and *Go South Young Man*. He tours the American military bases.

Tommy Dorsey, Bud Freeman, Pops Foster, Louis, Eddie Condon, Red Allen, and George Wettling at the Paramount Theater, New York.

1945

JANUARY Armstrong takes part in a concert organized by the Jazz Foundation of New Orleans. ■ He is booked at the Zanzibar, New York, through March. ■ **AUGUST–SEPTEMBER** California. He records "I Wonder" and "Jodie Man" with a studio band. Film: *Pillow to Post* by Vincent Sherman with Ida Lupino (Warner Bros.). ■ Makes regular appearances on radio shows sponsored by Coca-Cola.

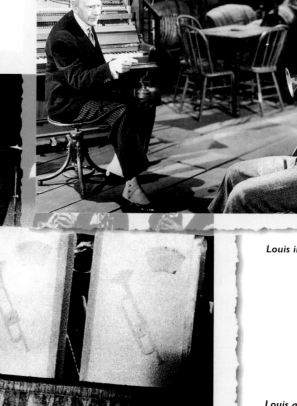

Louis in New Orleans.

Louis and his orchestra at the Aquarium, New York.

1946

SPRING–SUMMER Does stints in New York at the Aquarium (April–May), Apollo (June), and in Chicago at the Regal (June) and Savoy Ballroom (August). In Hollywood, he performs in Arthur Lubin's *New Orleans* (United Artists) alongside Barney Bigard, Kid Ory, Red Callender, Bud Scott, Charlie Beal, Zutty Singleton, and Billie Holliday. He later declares: "The things those Hollywood people make us do are always a sham."

1947

At the Hammam, h Pierre Dac, Paris, March 1948.

FEBRUARY 8 Concert at Carnegie Hall with the sextet of clarinetist Edmund Hall, at which Louis evokes the different stages of his career: New Orleans, Chicago, New York, and Hollywood. He also sings duets with Billie Holliday, backed by his big band, which is making what, due to the economic crisis, will be one of its last appearances. ■ **MAY 17** He gives a concert at the Town Hall in New York with a small band put together at his request by trumpet player Bobby Hackett: Jack Teagarden (trombone), George Wettling and Big Sid Catlett (drums), Dick Cary (piano), Peanuts Hucko (clarinet), Bob Hagart (bass). Louis suffers from polyps on the vocal chords. ■ **JUNE 9** The preview of the film *New Orleans* at the Winter Gardens is followed by a concert with the musicians from Armstrong's Town Hall formation. ■ **JULY** Louis goes into the hospital for a thorough check-up. Plays at the Apollo. ■ **AUGUST 13** The first outing for the new "All Stars" hired by Joe Glaser at Billy Berg's, Los Angeles: Jack Teagarden, Barney Bigard, Dick Cary, Arvell Shaw, Sid Catlett, and Velma Middleton. ■ **FALL** Concerts at the Chicago Civic Opera, New York Town Hall, and the Boston Symphony Hall. Live recordings are made of "Muskrat Ramble," "Black and Blue," "Royal Garden Blues," "Mahogany Hall Stomp." ■ Sees out the year at Billy Berg's Club. Publication in France of *Louis Armstrong, le roi du jazz* by Robert Goffin (Seghers) and *Louis Armstrong* by Hugues Panassié (Editions du Belvédère).

1948

JANUARY Dates at the Roxy Theater, New York. ■ In Paris, the French band leader Ray Ventura records Paul Misraki's song, "Armstrong, Duke Ellington, Cab Calloway." It features in the Jean Boyer film *Mademoiselle s'amuse.* ■ **FEBRUARY 22–28** Armstrong is in France with his All Stars for the jazz festival in Nice (Dick Cary is replaced by Earl Hines): "An indescribable triumph." Represented by Yves Montand, the French President, Vincent Auriol, presents Louis with a vase in Sèvres china. Louis gives two

Louis and the French singer Yves Montand at the Nice festival.

concerts at the Salle Pleyel, March 2 and 3. ■ **MAY** Returns to the United States. Plays at Carnegie Hall and takes part in the first Dixieland Jubilee. ■ **OCTOBER** More films: *Courtin' Trouble* by Ford Beebe (Monogram) and *A Song Is Born* by Howard Hawks, with Danny Kaye (RKO). "The result was atrocious from beginning to end," admitted Hawks later. "The only good surprise was that Satchmo and I became such great pals."

1949

JANUARY Louis plays at Governor Adlai Stevenson's inauguration ball. Concerts in Vancouver and Louisiana (February). ■ **FEBRUARY 21** Louis Armstrong makes the cover of *Time*. ■ **MARCH 1** In keeping with the old Mardi Gras tradition in New Orleans, Louis is elected "King of the Zulus" and is pulled through the streets on a float. He is made an honorary citizen. ■ **SEPTEMBER** Temporary engagements at the Flamingo, Las Vegas, then in Chicago, Detroit, and New York. ■ Records "Blueberry Hill" and "That Lucky Old Sun" with Gordon Jenkins's band and "My Sweet Hunk O' Trash" and "You Can't Lose a Broken Heart" with Billie Holliday. ■ **OCTOBER–NOVEMBER** European tour with Jack Teagarden, Barney Bigard, Earl Hines, Arvell Shaw, and Cozy Cole. ■ In Rome, Louis and Lucille are given a private audience by the Pope. "We don't have a child, but we keep trying!"

Louis, "King of the Zulus."

TIME

THE WEEKLY NEWSMAGAZINE

LOUIS ARMSTRONG
When you got to ask what it is, you never get to know.
(Music)

1950

APRIL Touring in the United States and Canada. ■ Records "Panama," "New Orleans Function," "Bugle Call Rag." ■ **JUNE** Records "La Vie en Rose" and "C'est si bon," songs by Édith Piaf, which he heard while on tour in Belgium. ■ **JULY** On the official date of Louis' fiftieth birthday, *Down Beat* and *The Record Changer* produce a special Louis Armstrong issue.

1951

JANUARY Recording of a concert in Pasadena: "Indiana," "Baby It's Cold Outside," "My Monday Date," "You Can Depend On Me." ■ Films: *The Strip* by Leslie Kardos, with Mickey Rooney (MGM), *Here Comes the Groom* by Frank Capra, with Bing Crosby and Jane Wyman (Paramount), and *Botta e Riposta* by Mario Soldati, with Fernandel.

Louis and Lucille Armstrong.

1952

JANUARY Plays in *Glory Alley* by Raoul Walsh with Leslie Caron, Ralph Meeker, and Gilbert Roland (MGM). ■ Records: "Kiss of Fire," "I'll Walk Alone." ■ Meets Frank Sinatra on the *Edsel Show* "Birth of the Blues." ■ **FEBRUARY–MARCH** Does a week-long booking in Sacramento, California. Plays six concerts in Honolulu. Dates in San Francisco and Vancouver. ■ **APRIL–MAY** Concerts at the universities of Arizona, Illinois, and Wisconsin. Then in Detroit, Toronto, and Montreal. The *Down Beat* readers' poll elects him "the most important musical figure of all time" (Duke Ellington comes second, J. S. Bach seventh). ■ **JUNE–JULY** Does four weeks at the Blue Note, Chicago, then at the Paramount, New York. The trombone player Trummy Young joins the All Stars. ■ **NOVEMBER** Embarks on another European tour with Trummy Young, Bob McCracken (clarinet), Arvell Shaw (bass), Marty Napoleon (piano), and Cozy Cole (drums), taking in Scandinavia, Germany, Switzerland, Italy, Belgium, France, and North Africa. ■ At Cinecitta, Louis plays in a musical sketch for *La Route du Bonheur*, a film by Maurice Labro, in which Django Reinhardt and Sidney Bechet also make appearances. ■ Publication of *Ma Nouvelle Orléans*, a French translation of the first and only volume of his biography, covering the years 1900–22 (Julliard, translation by Madeleine Gautier). The American edition follows two years later.

The Glenn Miller Story, with James Stewart. Left to right: Trummy Young, Louis Armstrong, Cozy Cole, Gene Krupa, Barney Bigard, Arvel Shaw, and Marty Napoléon.

1953

APRIL Concert tour with Benny Goodman. There is an open conflict between the two leaders and the two men split. ■ **FALL–WINTER** Triumphant tour of Japan where "huge crowds come to applaud him."

1954

JULY 12–14 In Chicago, records songs by W. C. Handy with his All Stars: "Saint Louis Blues," "Yellow Dog Blues," "The Memphis Blues," "Long Gone." According to his faithful companion, the clarinetist Barney Bigard, now back in the band, this is "Armstrong's favorite record." ■ **AUGUST** The Black magazine *Ebony* publishes an article by Louis entitled "Why I Like Dark Women," in which he writes: "I like women pretty, tender and dark—the darker the fruit, the sweeter the juice!" ■ **FALL** Australian tour. Film: *The Glenn Miller Story* by Anthony Mann with James Stewart and June Allyson (Universal International). Stewart recalls: "During the shoot, I had the best jazz teacher in all America: Louis Armstrong. That incredible man really is jazz personified." ■ American publication of Louis' autobiography, *Satchmo, My Life in New Orleans* (Prentice-Hall, New York).

African Tour, Accra, 1956.

1955

JANUARY 21 At the Crescendo Club, a Hollywood cabaret, Louis records "When It's Sleepy Time Down South" (his signature tune), "My Bucket's Got a Hole in It," "Don't Fence Me," "Rockin' Chair," and "The Whiffenpoof Song" (a blast at the Beeboppers). ■ **SPRING** Plays at Basin Street, New York. Records Fats Waller's most famous themes: "Black and Blue," "Ain't Misbehavin'," "All That Meat and No Potatoes," "Honeysuckle Rose," "Squeeze Me" (April 26–27). ■ **SEP-TEMBER 28** Records one of his biggest hits, "Mack the Knife" (from Brecht and Weill's *Threepenny Opera*). ■ **SEPTEMBER–DECEMBER** European tour: Scandinavia, Germany, Belgium, Switzerland, France, Italy (in Milan he records a few tracks for the album *Ambassador Satch*), Spain. ■ Edmund Hall replaces Barney Bigard.

Louis and W. C. Handy in the Columbia Records studio.

1956

Louis performs with the All Stars at Carnegie Hall and the Fox Theater in Brooklyn. Records with Ella Fitzgerald: "Stars Fell on Alabama," "Tenderly," "April in Paris," "Moonlight in Vermont." Tours Australia and the Far East. ■

MAY–JUNE Tours England (he is applauded by the Royal Family at the Empress Hall in London), Scotland, and Ireland, then on to Africa. He is greeted at Accra airport, Gold Coast, by a raucously enthusiastic crowd of ten thousand. "After all, this is where my ancestors came from, and I still have African blood in my veins." ■

JULY 14 Plays "Saint Louis Blues" with the Lewisohn Stadium Symphony Orchestra in New York, conducted by Leonard Bernstein. ■ **FALL** Plays at Paree, Chicago. ■

DECEMBER 18 Plays in the benefit concert for the Hungary Support Fund at the Royal Festival Hall in London, where Sir Laurence Olivier introduces him as follows: "Listen as this admirable, this noble man —for that is what he is—gives us a sample of pure music." ■ Film: *High Society* by Charles Walters with Bing Crosby, Frank Sinatra, and Grace Kelly (MGM). He plays "High Society," "Calypso," and "Now You Has Jazz," accompanied by his All Stars.

Louis and Grace Kelly in High Society.

Louis (middle) with Lionel Hampton (left) and Dizzy Gillespie (right).

1957

JANUARY In New York, Louis records new versions of his old hits for a four-record set produced by Milt Gabler and entitled *Satchmo, A Musical Autobiography*: "I Can't Give You Anything But Love," "Lazy River," "When You're Smiling," "Georgia On My Mind," "That's My Home," "Song of the Islands," "Cornet Chop Suey," "King of the Zulus," "Two Deuces," "You Rascal You." Each selection is preceded by a brief commentary by Louis. ■

FEBRUARY 19 In Knoxville, Tennessee, racists throw dynamite from their car outside the municipal theater where Louis is giving a concert. "Don't worry," he tells the audience, "it's only the telephone." ■ **MARCH** During the independence celebrations in Ghana, Lucille Armstrong, as the guest of President Nkrumah, attends the premiere of *Saga of Satchmo*, a film of Louis' recent tour made by Edward R. Murrow for CBS. ■ **APRIL** Plays at the Roxy, New York. ■ **MAY** Gives a concert in Kingston, Jamaica in front of an audience of 100,000, then tours the eastern United States. ■ **JULY 4** Louis' birthday is celebrated at the Newport Jazz Festival, which he headlines. He plays for 25,000 spectators at Lewisohn Stadium, Harlem, and with Lionel Hampton's band at the Atlantic City Festival. ■ **SEPTEMBER** When the State Department asks him to undertake a tour of the USSR as

Recording "Autobiography."

an "artistic ambassador," Armstrong tells a journalist at Grand Forks, North Dakota (where he is giving a concert) that he refuses to represent the United States abroad: "If people over there ask me what's going on in my country, what am I to tell them? Things are so bad in the United States that it's like the Blacks don't even have a homeland. In Little Rock, Arkansas, they just used the National Guard to prevent Black children from going to school. President Eisenhower may have no stomach, but he has two faces. He allowed Governor Faubus to go against the Federal Government. As for Faubus, he's just a fool. If that's the way they treat my brothers, I will not go to the USSR. If the government lets them persecute the Blacks, it can go to hell!" The FBI, which has kept a file on him since 1948, carefully records his various statements condemning segregation. ■ **NOVEMBER** On tour in South America, Louis triumphs in Brazil (where President Kubitschek gives a banquet in his honor), Argentina, Uruguay, and Venezuela. "In Caracas we played in a huge arena and Trummy [Young] and I did an imitation bullfight." ■ Back to New York for the end of the year. Television appearances.

Louis at the Victoria Hall, Geneva, 1955.

1958

FEBRUARY Tours the Midwest. Records gospel: *Louis and the Good Book*—"Nobody Knows," "Down By The Riverside," "Shadrak," "Swing Low," "Go Down Moses." ■ **MAY** Concerts in Montreal with the All Stars. ■ **JULY** At the Newport Festival, where the photographer Bern Stern makes *Jazz on a Summer's Day*, Louis plays "Lazy River," "Tiger Rag," "When the Saints," and "Rockin' Chair." Concerts at Lewisohn Stadium, Harlem, and Hampstead (Long Island), not far from his home in Corona, where he takes a few days' rest. ■ **SEPTEMBER–OCTOBER** Television show in Hollywood with Bing Crosby. Records *Satchmo Plays King Oliver* with his regular band: "Saint James Infirmary Blues," "Panama," "Doctor Jazz," "Frankie and Johnny," "Chimes Blues." ■ **NOVEMBER** Tours Pennsylvania. Film: *The Five Pennies* by Melville Shavelson, with Danny Kaye (Paramount).

Louis, Erroll Garner, and Coleman Hawkins at Newport, 1958.

Arriving at the Newport Festival in 1958 (left: George Wein).

1959

JANUARY 7 Performs "Umbrella Man" with Dizzy Gillespie for *The Timex Jazz TV Show*. ■ **MID-JANUARY–MAY** Undertakes a major international tour: Scandinavia (in Denmark, he makes an appearance in the film *Kaerlighedens Melodi,* [The Formula of Love]), Holland, Germany (more films: *Die Nacht vor der Premiere* by Georg Jakoby, and *La Paloma* by Paul Martin), Switzerland, Austria, England, Belgium, Greece, Turkey, France, and Italy. ■ **JUNE** He recovers from pneumonia he contracted in Spoleto, the gravity of which is exaggerated in the press. In a letter to a French friend, he describes a dream he had during his illness: "Old Bechet, Bid Sid Catlett and all the 'cats' up there tried to get me along to play first trumpet, but they only wanted to pay union rates, so I said 'Better luck next time!' Ha! Ha! Ha!" ■ Back to the States. ■ **JULY 4** For his concert at Lewisohn Stadium, he is greeted by a tremendous rendering of "Happy Birthday" by the ten thousand spectators. ■ **DECEMBER** Protesting against the race laws promulgated in Louisiana, which formally prohibit white and black musicians from playing in the same band, as they do in his own group, Armstrong declares: "All around the world I get treated better than in my home town. Jazz was born there and I remember a time when it wasn't a crime for musicians of different colors to play together.... I'm going back to New Orleans just to get beaten up by Whites." ■ Concert at Carnegie Hall. ■ Film: *The Beat Generation* by Charles Haas, with Steve Cochran (MGM).

1960

JUNE Concerts at Madison Square Garden, New York, and in Canada. ■ **JULY–AUGUST** Newport Festival. Concerts in Tuxedo and Washington. ■ **OCTOBER** African tour. In Ghana, when the dean of Accra University asks him about his music, he replies: "There are those who get jazz and those who don't, it's as simple as that." The tour proceeds through Nigeria, Douala, Brazzaville, Nairobi, Zanzibar, Dar es Salaam, Salisbury, Elisabethville (where six thousand Katangas give him an almost hysterical welcome in an open-air sports ground), Leopoldville, Guinea, and Ivory Coast. But he is refused entry into South Africa, where the Minister of Foreign Affairs considers that "It is not in the country's interest, at the present time, to authorize a visit by Armstrong." ■ When a journalist asks him what he is trying to prove with this African tour, he replies: "I'm not trying to prove anything at all. I'm going there to blow into my trumpet. I'm ready to play wherever there are people who love my music. And one day I'd like to slip behind the Iron Curtain! The summit meetings they have with all those ministers don't seem to be getting anywhere much. Perhaps old Satchmo could achieve something with his trumpet at a little conference in the basement." ■ **DECEMBER** Concerts in Paris; Martin Ritt shoots *Paris Blues* (music by Duke Ellington), with Paul Newman, Joan Woodward, and Sidney Poirier (United Artists).

The African Tour.

1961

FEBRUARY During the second part of the African tour, the singer Velma Middleton dies in Freetown (Sierra Leone). ■ Back to France for two concerts in Nice, then to Switzerland. ■ **APRIL** Booked at Basin Street East, New York. ■ Records with Duke Ellington, playing the latter's compositions: "It Don't Mean A Thing," "Do Nothing Till You Hear From Me," "Black and Tan," "The Mooche," "Cotton Tail." ■ **SUMMER** Newport and Randall's Island festivals, concert at the Music Circus, Lambertville. ■ Records with Dave Brubeck. ■ **DECEMBER** Plays once again at Basin Street East.

Louis and Lotte Lenya
recording **The Threepenny Opera.**

1962

MARCH–MAY Tours Germany, Austria, France, Switzerland, England, Spain, Portugal, and Holland with Trummy Young, Joe Darensbourg (clarinet), Billy Kyle (piano), Billy Cronk (bass), Danny Barcelona (drums), and Jewell Brown (vocals). ■ **JULY** Newport Festival. Guest of honor on the *Ed Sullivan Show*. ■ **OCTOBER** Concerts in California and neighboring states. ■ Plays in the traditional jazz festival Dixieland at Disneyland (Anaheim, California). Kid Ory and Johnny St. Cyr from the original Hot Five group join Louis to play "Muskrat Ramble" in the short film *Disneyland by Night*. ■ Private trip to Egypt, where he poses with Lucille in front of the sphinx at Gizeh.

The Switzerland tour.

1963

MARCH Touring New Zealand, Australia, South Korea, Hong Kong, Tokyo, Manila. ■ **MAY 22** Louis plays at the Waldorf Astoria, New York, at a dinner given in honor of President Kennedy. He leads a band comprising Ed Sullivan, Eddie Fisher, Mel Ferrer, Henry Fonda, and Tony Randall. Tours Iowa, Massachusetts, and New Jersey. ■ **SEPTEMBER** Engagement at the Club Riviera, Las Vegas. ■ **DECEMBER** After a concert at Smith College, Massachusetts, he sings "God Bless America," *a capella,* in homage to President Kennedy, who was assassinated in Dallas nine days earlier. ■ Records "Hello Dolly," the signature tune of a new musical on Broadway.

1964

JANUARY After eleven years with the band, Trummy Young quits, tired out by constant touring. He is replaced by the Pima Indian Big Chief Moore. ■ **MARCH** Louis spends a week at the Beth Israel Hospital, New York, for treatment of paraphlebitis. The newspapers run reports of a "heart attack." ■ **APRIL 8** Records the LP *Hello Dolly! This Is Armstrong*. The single, "Hello Dolly," rises to the number-one slot in the hit parades. The loudspeakers on Broadway play it all day long, as does the radio. The *New York Post* estimates that the record is played ten thousand times a day on the American continent! ■ **JULY 2** The New York Fair organizes an "Armstrong Day," during which he is awarded a commemorative medal. ■ **AUGUST** Hyannis Festival (Massachusetts). ■ **SEPTEMBER 3** Records "So Long Dearie" and "Pretty Little Missy." ■ **NOVEMBER 3** "Faith" and "Bye and Bye." ■ **DECEMBER** The South African government refuses to grant Louis a visa. Armstrong: "It's more their loss than mine." ■ Does a TV show and tours Japan.

Louis writing letters in Corona.

1965

JANUARY 1 Gives a concert for prisoners at San Quentin, California. Tours Minnesota and gives the inaugural ball for President Johnson at the White House. ■ Ten-day engagement in Framingham, a suburb of Boston. Back to New York for a TV show, the *Bell Telephone Hour*. ■ **FEBRUARY 5** Concert in Halifax, Nova Scotia. Three-day tour around Iceland. ■ Concerts in the West Indies and Miami. Tyree Glenn replaces Big Chief Moore. *International Musician* announces that Louis may play the music for a mass "approved by the Vatican." ■ **MARCH 5** Concert at Carnegie Hall with Leopold Stokowski. ■ **MARCH 12** Sets off on a tour of the popular democracies: Prague, Leipzig, East Berlin. "After Berlin we went to Bucharest where they have a marvelous theater. The evenings in Yugoslavia were fantastic too. Then back to East Berlin and on to Magdeburg, Erfurt, Schwerin. In Barth they showed us the place where the grandparents of Bix Beiderbecke lived, a hundred years ago." ■ At a press conference at Copenhagen Airport, he comments on the racist violence in Selma, Alabama. "On television I saw how the police in Selma beat women and children. It made me feel sick. How can human beings treat their fellow creatures like that? They'd hit Jesus if he were black and fainting in the street.... Luther King, whom I know very well, is a magnificent man. But my mission is music. If I demonstrated, they'd smash my face in so I couldn't play the trumpet any more." ■ **APRIL 9** Returns to the United States. Television pays tribute to his "fifty years in show business." Edward G. Robinson reads a message from Senator Jacob K. Javits: "The Communist newspapers spoke about Armstrong on their front pages. Such is the success of this artist so richly endowed with talent and humanity that he has won over countless nations and races around the world. He deserves the thanks of the U.S. government." ■ **JUNE** New European tour: London, Manchester, Paris, Stockholm, Malmö (where he is made Honorary Fireman), Copenhagen, Helsinki, and Budapest—then back to the United States for two small movie parts: *When the Boys Meet the Girls* by Alvin Genser, with Connie Francis and Paul Anka (MGM), and *A Man Called Adam* by Leo Pen, alongside Sammy Davis Jr. (Embassy Pictures), who declares: "I'm there to give it my all, because I'm the star, and then they show a close-up of Louis and suddenly it turns into a Louis Armstrong movie." ■ **JULY 4** Official celebration of his sixty-fifth birthday. Messages of friendship and gratitude flood in from all parts of the globe. He is awarded the Freedom Medal by the U.S. government. ■ He begins a two-week engagement at the Steel Peer, Atlantic City, on this same day. ■ **AUGUST** A week in Toronto, then Portland and Boston. ■ **SEPTEMBER** A short stay in New Orleans to give a benefit concert for the Jazz Museum. He is greeted by his old teacher from the Waif's Home, Peter Davis. A grand street parade is organized in his honor. ■ **DECEMBER 2** He celebrates his fifty years in the business at Carnegie Hall, where he is voted "Man of the Year" by the American Guild of Variety Artists.

*Louis in Paris
with French policemen.*

1966

FEBRUARY Death of Louis' pianist and friend Billy Kyle. ■ **MAY** Records "Cabaret" and "Mame." "An American Genius" is the title of a fifteen-page article in *Life* magazine (May 16). In Los Angeles he sings in honor of Prince Philip, the Duke of Edinburgh. He plays with his "favorite band," the Guy Lombardo orchestra, for the first time. ■ **JULY–SEPTEMBER** Summer season at the Jones Beach Marine Theater. ■ Tours and television shows through the end of the year.

1967

APRIL 23 Bronchio-pneumonia forces Louis to cancel his engagements for the coming months. ■ **JULY 26–27** Fully recovered, he plays at the Festival d'Antibes. Jean-Christophe Averty films the two concerts for French television. Next stops: Dublin and Majorca. ■ **AUGUST** In New York, he records "What a Wonderful World," "The Sunshine of Love," "Hellzapoppin'." ■ **SEPTEMBER** He falls ill once more and has to break off an engagement in Reno, Nevada. He is able to return home to Corona on September 28. ■ **OCTOBER–DECEMBER** Recording sessions. Songs include "Mi va di Cantara," "Grassa bella," "Farfalina," "Dimmi dimmi," and "No Time and We're a Home" (with the All Stars and Clark Terry).

1968

FEBRUARY 1–3 With Lionel Hampton, plays at the San Remo Festival. He is given an audience with the Pope, after which he declares: "I am a Baptist, my wife is a Catholic, I wear a Star of David for luck and the Pope is my friend." ■ **MARCH** Back on the road (Pennsylvania, Maine, New York) with a two-week engagement in Mexico City. Makes *Hello Dolly*, the musical by Gene Kelly with Barbra Streisand (20th Century Fox). Records "Sunrise," "Talk To The Animals," and "I Will Wait For You," from Jacques Demy's film *The Umbrellas of Cherbourg*. ■ **JUNE** Appears at the New Orleans Jazz Fest. Tours England, playing at the Variety Club, Batley, Yorkshire (from June 17) and in Leeds, then London in early July. ■ **SEPTEMBER** Louis convalesces after a stay in the hospital for phlebitis. "Just the sight of my schedule makes me tired. And yet Joe Glaser, who has been my manager for thirty-six years, keeps turning down bookings. I play the trumpet 350 days a year! It's true that the trumpet comes first, before even my wife.... When I retire for real I'll spend my time helping youngsters the way I myself was helped. There are so many things I'll do, like going to hear other musicians, visit with friends, stay at home and enjoy my wife's good cooking. That's the life."

1969

FEBRUARY Heart problems and a kidney infection keep him at the Beth Israel Hospital, New York until April. A tracheotomy is performed. European radio stations announce Louis' death. ■ **JUNE** Death of Joe Glaser at Beth Israel (June 6). Louis sings at a charity benefit for the trumpeter Louis Metcalf. ■ **AUGUST** Performs with Duke Ellington at the Rainbow Grill, New York. ■ **OCTOBER** Records "We Have All The Time In The World," the theme tune for the Bond movie *Her Majesty's Secret Service.* ■ Film: *L'Aventure du Jazz* by Louis and Claudine Panassié. Louis is interviewed at home in Corona, in the borough of Queens (New York) and talks about New Orleans, the blues, segregation, and…cassoulet. ■ Appears on *The Andy Williams Show* on TV. Gives a few concerts with the All Stars.

Louis and Barbra Streisand in **Hello Dolly.**

1970

APRIL The New Orleans Jazz and Heritage Festival is dedicated to "the town's most famous son." Louis gives a concert with Dizzy Gillespie and Bobby Hackett. ■ **MAY 13** Duke Ellington records "Portrait of Louis Armstrong" as part of his *New Orleans Suite*. ■ **MAY 29** Louis records the album *Louis Armstrong and His Friends* for Bob Thiele's Flying Dutchman label, with arrangements by Oliver Nelson. Louis sings a mixed bag of themes: John Lennon's "Give Peace A Chance," Ellington's "Mood Indigo," "The Creator Has A Master Plan" by Pharaoh Sanders, and a protest song, "We Shall Overcome" (recorded with a choir). At the end of the session, Louis declares: "I never felt better. The doctors are going to tell me I can play the trumpet again. Actually—shhh!—I already do play a little every evening." Miles Davis, Ornette Coleman,

Louis and his wife, Lucille.

Chico Hamilton, Leon Thomas, Tony Bennett, and Eddie Condon sit in on the sessions and get the birthday celebrations rolling early. ■ **JULY 3** Louis gives a concert at the Shrine Auditorium, Los Angeles, during which the composer Hoagy Carmichael, as master of ceremonies, presents Satchmo with a birthday cake. Dizzy Gillespie pays homage at the Monterey Festival. "If it weren't

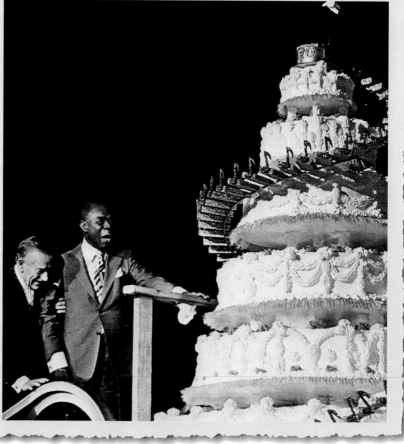

Louis and Hoagy Carmichael: Los Angeles, July 3, 1970.

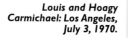

for Louis, none of us would be here today." July 10 is Armstrong Day at Newport. Six trumpeters—Dizzy Gillespie, Bobby Hackett, Joe Newman, Wild Bill Davidson, Jimmy Owens, and Ray Nance—each play a piece by Louis symbolizing a different stage of his career. "Without Louis, none of us would be here," declares Gillespie. Film: *Trumpet Players Tribute* by George Wein and Sidney J. Stiber. Armstrong: "Some critics say I'm a clown, but clowns are great. What a joy it is to make people happy. When I play, I just think about the good times... and the notes come of their own accord. You have to love to be able to play." ■ **AUGUST** Records the album *Country and Western Armstrong*. ■ **SEPTEMBER** At the International Hotel in Las Vegas, where they are recording "The Pearl Bailey Show with Louis Armstrong as Special Guest," Louis plays the trumpet in public for the first time in two years. He plays and sings at a charity gala in London on October 29. ■ **DECEMBER 26** Returns to Las Vegas for a two-week engagement.

Dizzy Gillespie at the Monterey Festival.

1971

FEBRUARY 10 *David Frost Show* with Bing Crosby. ■ **MARCH** Two weeks at the Waldorf Astoria. Louis has to be helped on stage. ■ He is hospitalized at Beth Israel (March 15) for a lung infection and heart problems. His doctors have to use a respirator. After an operation a week later, there are signs of improvement. He can start eating again. After seven weeks of care, he goes home to his little white house in Corona on May 6. ■ **JUNE 23** Gives a press conference from home to thank all those who sent get-well messages and to show them that he is better. He plays four tunes on his trumpet, including his favorite theme, "Sleepy Time Down South." "I'll be back to work as soon as my legs are as fit as my lips." ■ **JULY 6** Louis dies in his sleep at 5:30 in the morning. "Heart failure," diagnoses his doctor. He leaves $300,000 to his widow, Lucille, $5,000 to his sister, Beatrice Collins, and $5,000 to his cousin, Clarence Hatfield. President Nixon pays homage to "this architect of American art whose great talent and magnificent spirit have enriched our lives." ■ **JULY 8** The trumpet player Charlie Shavers dies of cancer at age fifty-four. His last wish, that his trumpet should be buried with Satchmo, is granted by Lucille. ■ Between 10 a.m. and 10 p.m., thousands of admirers file past him as he lies in state at the armory of the 7th Infantry Regiment on Park Avenue. He rests in a bronze coffin in a dark suit and pink shirt, with a big white handkerchief in his hand. ■ **JULY 9** The funeral is held at the Congregational Church of Corona and broadcast by satellite to sixteen countries. The many musicians in attendance include Ella Fitzgerald, Duke Ellington, Benny Goodman, Lionel Hampton, Dizzy Gillespie, Earl Hines, Bing Crosby, Frank Sinatra, Sarah Jones, Gene Krupa, and Guy Lombardo. The service is conducted by Reverend Robert D. Sherard, who insists on "Armstrong's message to the younger generations." The funeral oration is given by Fred Robbins, a New York disc jockey and old friend, who tells the Archangel Gabriel that he can make ready to welcome Satchmo, "an authentic American popular hero." After the crowd has paid its respects, the coffin is transported to Flushing Cemetery, Corona. On the plaque, Lucille simply engraves: "Louis Armstrong Satchmo." ■ **AUGUST 29** Death of Lil Hardin-Armstrong, aged seventy-three, from a heart attack during a concert in Chicago. ■ **SEPTEMBER–OCTOBER** The junction of 108th Street and Northern Boulevard in Corona is renamed Louis Armstrong Memorial Square. ■ Louis' last recording, "It Was The Night Before Christmas," a poem read to music, is published by the Lorillard Tobacco Company and given out free in supermarkets. The Republic of Chad issues a series of three stamps with the images of black musicians: Sidney Bechet (50F), Duke Ellington (75F), and Louis Armstrong (100F). Senegal, Mali, Rwanda, and Niger also issue stamps with Armstrong's effigy.

Preceding page: Louis and Joséphine Baker.

Following page: Park Avenue Armory, New York.

1973

JULY 4 The new Louis Armstrong Memorial Stadium (formerly the Singer Bowl) is inaugurated in New York with a "Tribute to Louis Armstrong" featuring some fifty musicians in the presence of Lucille Armstrong. ■ With Tyree Glenn, Lucille writes a memoir entitled *Louis and Me*. ■ A national subscription is started to raise a statue in New Orleans (The Louis Armstrong Statue Fund, president: Benny Carter).

1974

JULY A bust of Louis Armstrong is inaugurated in the Jardins de Cimiez, Nice, in the presence of Lucille and Princess Grace of Monaco. ■ The City's Grand Jazz Parade celebrates the memory of the "master" from July 15–21. ■ Paramount announces a film about Louis' life.

Statue of Louis, at the Louis Armstrong Park in New Orleans.

1980

APRIL Inauguration of the Louis Armstrong Park in New Orleans, and of the statue on the site of the old Congo Square, where the descendants of the slaves used to congregate with their African drums at the end of the nineteenth century.

Medal from the Mint of Paris.

1998

JUNE 20 Inauguration of Place Louis Armstrong in Paris' 13th arrondissement. This square is alongside the rue Jenner, the location of Polydor studios, where Louis Armstrong took part in a recording session in 1934.

Lucille and Princess Grace of Monaco during the inauguration of Armstrong's statue in Nice.

the tr o

" I come

rumpets
i fame

"When you suddenly hear
those old Louis Armstrong masterpieces
spruced up, washed and scrubbed and
polished, rejuvenated, you realize that,
perhaps after all, there has never been
anything so exciting, so reckless, so virtuoso,
so bold, so lyrical, so crazy, so beautiful."

Maurice Henry

"The simple sight of nasturtiums in a courtyard window threw me into a sudden rapture, thunderstruck by the still lightning of their orange. Armstrong, the Pan of Paris, was shaking up the gray walls of the everyday with his trumpet and the whole town was dancing round his petals of fire."

André Hardellet
Paris des poètes

"My father was born in New Orleans and was a young man when Louis Armstrong did errands for the joints in what has always been presented to me as one of the most perverse of cities. Even today, when I think of New Orleans, I can't help thinking of Sodom and Gomorrah. My father never spoke to me of Louis Armstrong, except to forbid us to listen to his records. And yet for years we had a portrait of him on our wall. A particularly energetic friend of my father's had put it there and forbidden him to touch it."

James Baldwin

"The first bars of Armstrong's solo on 'Tight Like This' can awaken a sense of the sublime. In them he reveals all the hostility and all the sadness of the world with what could be called a dramatic serenity, and the phrasing is enwrapped in the glow, the grandiose aura, the glory of a matchless sound."

Lucien Malson
Jazz-Hot

"Armstrong was going to improvise with his trumpet, to build a whole composition to which each note would be important and would contain within itself the essence of the whole. I was not disappointed: the atmosphere warmed up very fast. The scaffolding and flying buttresses of the jazz instruments supported Armstrong's trumpet.... The sounds of the trumpet sometimes piled up together, fusing a new musical base, a sort of matrix which gave birth to one precise, unique note, tracing a sound whose path was almost painful, so absolutely necessary had its equilibrium and duration become. It tore at the nerves of those who followed it. My heart began to accelerate…"

Marie Cardinale
Les Mots pour le dire

"Louis' 'West End Blues' introduction consists of only two phrases [...] these two phrases alone almost summarize Louis' entire style and his contribution to jazz language [...] The way Louis attacks each note, the quality and exact duration of each pitch, the manner in which he releases the note, and the subsequent split-second silence before the next note—in other words, the entire acoustical pattern—present in capsule form all the essential characteristics of jazz inflection."

Gunther Schuller
Early Jazz

"Louis is jazz in person, he's the creator of our language on the trumpet. It's impossible to say what he means to us. He is everything or almost everything, just on his own. To speak his name is to conjure up our whole world. No sentences. The name is enough."

Dizzy Gillespie
Down Beat

Louis and Dizzy Gillespie.

"Those first three notes Armstrong blew on his trumpet at his first concert in Paris after the Liberation, 'in flesh and blood.' Like a sweet swig of liquor in the bitter cold of winter."

Claude Roy
Permis de séjour

"We talked about all the things we had been denied for four years. Was Louis Armstrong still alive?"

Simone Signoret
La nostalgie n'est plus ce qu'elle était

"Nobody had or will ever have such a great influence on the jazz trumpet. No one has ever matched Louis' sound, his phrasing, his power. Louis was the first modern jazz musician."

Roy Eldridge
Metronome

"Armstrong can start playing the Marseillaise on the tuba, tomorrow morning… drop his pants in front of the Arc de Triomphe, saw off the Vendôme Column, with a blue fork and eat oysters running through the Tuileries for all I care, he will still have cut (at least) three hundred unforgettable songs."

Boris Vian

"The finest record I know is the Okeh version of 'Mabel's Dream'. Armstrong's second voice behind King Oliver brings tears to my eyes. In July 1967, at Antibes, I filmed the whole of Armstrong s two concerts. I had high expectations of this meeting, but I just couldn't get near him because he was surrounded by an incredible gang of pimps! What I'd really have liked to do was to get him sitting down in a studio and talking. In 1968, in New York, I tried to make a program about him but there was nothing doing. The way the big American networks saw it, all he was good for was coming and rolling his eyes on some show. Like Hollywood, all they saw in Armstrong was a buffoon."

Jean-Christophe Averty

"On to Broadway, home of Armstrong, the black titan of the cry, of the apostrophe, of the burst of laughter, of thunder. He sings, he guffaws, he squirts sounds from his silver trumpet. He is mathematics, balance on a tightrope. He is Shakespearean, forgive me! Imperial, Armstrong makes his entrance. His voice is deep as an abyss, like a black hole. He bursts out laughing, he hollers and puts his trumpet to his mouth. With his brass he is by turns demonic, chatty and monumental, from one second to the next, following his staggering wit. This man is madly intelligent: he is a king."

Le Corbusier
Quand les cathédrales étaient blanches

"Once there was a land. And there were no walls and there were no orchards. There was just a Boogie Woogie man whose name was Agamemnon. After a time he gave birth to two sons—Epaminondas and Louis the Armstrong. Epaminondas was for war and civilization [...] Louis was for peace and joy [...]. Agamemnon, seeing that one of his sons had wisdom, brought him a golden torque, saying unto him: 'Go forth now and trumpet peace and joy everywhere!' [...] Louis put his thick loving lips to the golden torque and blew. He blew one great big sour note like a rat bustin' open and the tears came to his eyes and the sweat rolled down his neck. Louis felt that he was bringing peace and joy to all the world. He filled his lungs again and blew a molten note that reached so far into the blue it froze and hung in the sky like a diamond-pointed star."

Henry Miller
The Colossus of Maroussi

"Once there was Louis Armstrong blowing his beautiful top in the muds of New Orleans..."

Jack Kérouac
On the Road

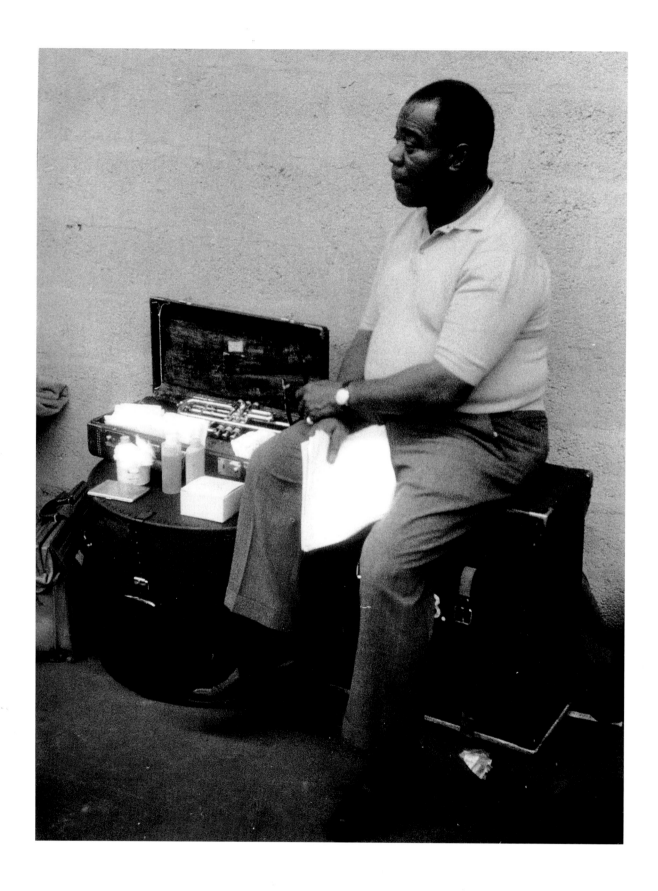

"Satchmo was singing 'Don t you play me cheap because I look so meek' and Babs was wriggling on Ronald's lap, excited by the way Satchmo sang it— the theme was sufficiently vulgar to take the kind of liberties that would have been unthinkable with 'Yellow Dog Blues', for example.... After the flaring trumpet, the yellow phallus cutting through the air and giving rhythm to the pleasure, then, towards the end, three hypnotically rising notes of pure gold, a perfect pause when all the swing in the world throbbed in one unbearable instant, then the shrill ejaculation, spurting and falling like a rocket in the sexual night..."

Julio Cortazar
Marelle

"...And when, a little tipsy after several little glasses of hastily downed cane sugar liquor, the verses of the Latin hymn:

*Dum esset
in accubitu suo,
Nardus mea dedit
odorem suavitis*

entered the dining room, we covered them with the ringing sounds of Louis Armstrong's trumpet broadcast by the radio."

Alejo Carpentier
Guerre du temps

Louis and Jean Cocteau, Nice, 1961.

"This is how, later, from all this frizzy blackness, we shall hear bursting out the death cry of Louis Armstrong, the man whose trumpet is unique. His trumpet speaks a kind of terrible human language, climbs, climbs in zigzags, pulls itself up, slides, and, without killing itself, reaches the top of the highest skyscraper, where it spits its jet of purple blood. Armstrong is the angel of Jericho, the soldier of the Apocalypse, the perfect point where the Negro's heavenly prayer meets his infernal eroticism."

Jean Cocteau

"He was still quite a way from Olivier's house. Suddenly he heard the trumpet of Louis Armstrong throwing out the pathetic chorus of 'Hobo You Can't Ride', his favorite blues. He stopped, stunned. Either he was hearing things or some other jazz lover owned the record too and was now entreating it to deliver him the enchantment, the exhilaration that it always lavished on Dodo. Leaning forward, his ears straining right then left, he listened. [...] Dodo, stock still in the velvety night—a casket of music—was now hearing the lustral waves of the trumpet's dizzying trills. What joy! An inhabitant of Vérannes, a stranger, but someone he would get to know, loved jazz and shared his admiration for the titan with copper lungs and a soul of crystal! Tomorrow, he would go and ring at the door of that house."

Louis and Charles Trénet.

"We left in the dark, around eleven or midnight, for the seaside. We played records, we danced.... Those were the nights I discovered jazz.... Armstrong. I became crazy about him."

Simenon
Un Homme comme les autres

Charles Trénet
Dodo Manières

"There is certainly a relation between my paintings and jazz music, especially Armstrong's. Above all, the works from 1942 and the years that followed. In those days I was mad about jazz and Armstrong, and in my mind I had paintings that were a kind of equivalent in terms of painting."

Jean Dubuffet

**Black Chicago,
by Jean Dubuffet**

"For me the sweet anger of Armstrong's trumpet, the froggy exuberance of his come-to-me-baby mouthings, are a piece of Proust's madeleine cake: they make Mississippi moons rise again, summon the muddy lights of river towns, the sound, like an alligator's yawn, of river horns."

Truman Capote
The Dogs Bark

CARE OF THE LIPS. "I've been playing thirty-seven years. When I was thirteen years old I was developing my lip, playing in the street parades. A man who's been playing his horn that long—not like some of these young trumpets today, they blow for two years, and they're through—figures to have some good advice to offer on the care of the lips and mouth. So here's a few words from Louis on that subject: look at Bunk—always had those buck teeth protruding, but just a year's dental work would have fixed him for life. But he never paid it any attention, and there were a whole lot of others like him. I watched all that and I profit by those people's mistakes. Every time I have two weeks off, the dentist is doing

something to my chops. I've got a good dentist, and by now the danger's gone; no more chance of pyor-rhea or anything. Also, a lot of trumpet players, their lips get tired and they don't make any effort to strengthen them. I put those spirits of nitrate on my lips every now and then. My mother used to put it in water and give it to us to drink for fever, when we were kids. (So I know if I slap a little of it on there, I'm not going to have any trouble blowing my horn. If there's any sharpness, any little sting, I'm going to put it on there, and I can blow my horn peaceful.) If your lips are not sore, you can put more force into it. But when you've got to pull your horn away, you're liable to miss a note, and you're liable to hurt yourself, too."

Louis Armstrong

"New Orleans is stirring,
rattling and sliding faintly in its fragrance
and in the enormous richness of its lust;
taxis are still parked along Dauphine Street
and the breastlike, floral air is itchy with
the stilettos and embroiderings above black
blood drumthroes of an eloquent cracked
indiscoverable cornet, which exists only
in the imagination and somewhere
in the past, in the broken heart
of Louis Armstrong."

James Agee
Let Us Now Praise Famous Men

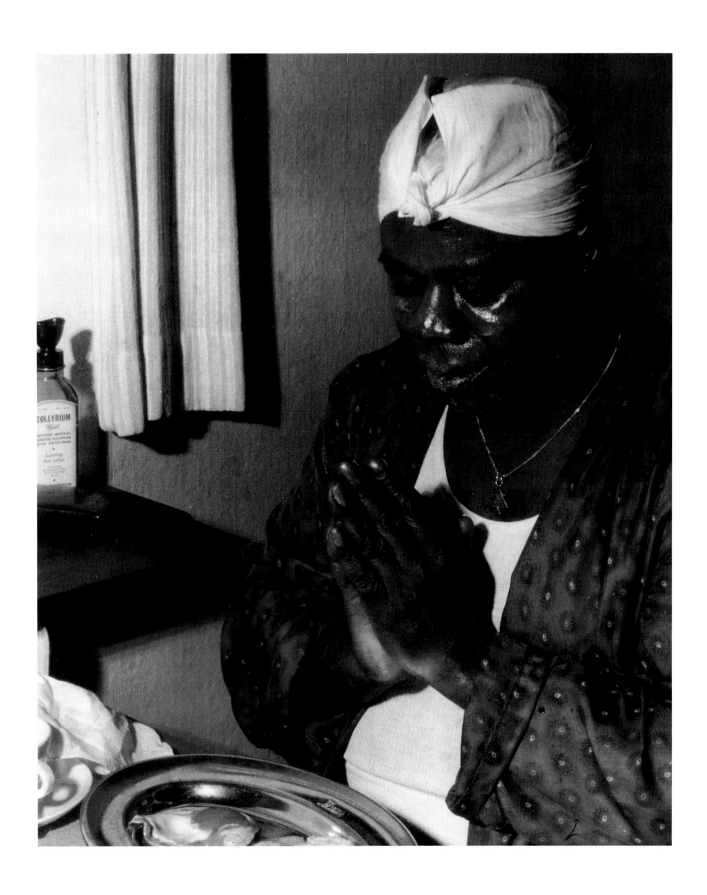

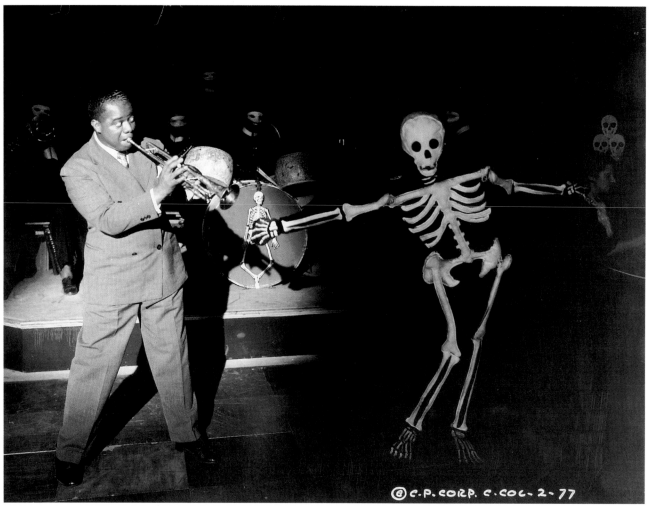

Louis in **Pennies from Heaven,** *1936.*

"...I can still remember the Hot Five with Lil
and Louis Armstrong. Honestly, they were quite incredible.
It was Louis who first made me realize that jazz was just as
rich a form of music as any other."

Nicholas Ray

Louis in **Goin' Places,** *1938.*

"[...] The only thing I regret about my film *High Society* is that they didn't let me develop the Cupid side of the Louis Armstrong character. You get the idea a bit when he plays and sings 'Samantha', and then when Grace Kelly hears him in her room. I wanted to make more of that idea, and the character, but 'they' refused, saying it wasn't worth it."

Charles Walters

"Louis is wonderful to work with. On any record we made together, I was really supporting Louis instead of vice versa."

Bing Crosby
Call Me Lucky

Louis in High Society
*by Charles Walters,
with Bing Crosby, Grace
Kelly, and Frank Sinatra.*

Louis in Goin' Places.

"It must have been in 1939. My brother and sister had bought the Armstrong records and they knocked us out."

Claude Sautet
Conversations with Claude Sautet

"After leaving the night-club Catherine and I, always in company with Jacques Becker, would go home and revel in interpretations of Red Nichols and Duke Ellington. Our hero was Louis Armstrong, 'Satchmo,' who was then quite young. He toured France with a band of half-a-dozen musicians [...]. I wondered how he would get on in the provinces. The first thing that caught my eye, when I arrived in Marseilles, was a placard announcing his appearance at the Palais de Cristal. That theatre is enormous, apart from which I could not believe that the Marseilles public was capable of understanding that kind of music. I was wrong. His visit was a triumph. [...] The audience applauded wildly for a performer of a kind quite new to them playing music that was utterly strange."

Jean Renoir
Ma vie et mes films

"— Can you give us your tastes in music? — I like, well, jazz, like Louis Armstrong."

Marilyn Monroe

"When I was very young, Louis Armstrong came to Prague. I ran after him to ask for an autograph. It's one of my greatest treasures, yes, absolutely!"

Milos Forman

Louis and Billie Holiday in **New Orleans, 1946.**

That Voice

That voice that sings in our desert
That voice that reminds us we are brothers
That voice that follows the beating of our hearts
That voice that offers the unknown
That voice that cancels space and time
The voice that reconciles us
That voice that is stronger than our dreams and nightmares
That voice that forces us to hear our hearts
That voice that accepts silence
That voice that unites heaven and hell
That voice that is the river of blood
The voice of Louis Armstrong.

Philippe Soupault

"Armstrong inspired thousands of trumpets, inspired countless vocations, enchanted millions of friends who, quite simply, listened. For me he's the epitome of the kind of American who goes beyond the rules, a truly good and original man."

Duke Ellington

"Nowadays Louis spends nearly all his time on the plane to Japan, Australia, Europe, spreading joy with his personality as much as with his music. A Louis Armstrong concert is synonymous with joy. Sometimes that gets him flack: austere critics have criticized him for being spectacular. But I say that there's no jazz worth listening to if it doesn't mix in a bit of humor; and that the music of Louis Armstrong has such charm, is so bewitching, that it's irresistible."

Duke Ellington

JAZZ

NOVEMBER-DECEMBER, 1962 • 50 CENTS

BUCK CLAYTON'S STORY

A NIGHT WITH MINGUS

3 ELLINGTON FIRSTS

Record Reviews • Jazz Puzzles • News

The Real Ambassador and Friend

hot-REVUE

Louis Armstrong

ÉRO 5   REVUE MENSUELLE DE JAZZ-HOT   AVRIL 1946

jazz
RYTM I PIOSENKA

Nr 9 (90)   Rok XVI
WRZESIEŃ 1971
LIL HARDIN
MAX JONES
L. FEATHER
M. ŚWIĘCICKI
o ARMSTRONGU

FEBRUAR 1946 . 90 Ø

JAZZinformation

Tribune

APRIL 1958 35c

Metronome

MUSIC USA
and
JAZZ today

B.G. and Louis
The Big Bands
Records

Nat Hentoff
Music Course
Jazz Thesis

CANADA'S JAZZ MAGAZINE
AUGUST 1973   15TH ANNIVERSARY ISSUE

coda

75 CENTS

A SPECIAL ISSUE
CELEBRATING
THE GENIUS OF
LOUIS ARMSTRONG

norsk Jazz

COUNT BASIE kommer 6. sept.
Gode platetips i annonsespaltene
3 sider fotos — nyheter — artikler

norsk JAZZ

8

LOUIS ARMSTRONG

afi: ANTON BRUEHL
FAIR

JAZZREVY

50 øre

ecember 1935 — 1. Aargang

LE ROI DU JAZZ
Louis Armstrong

LOUIS ARMSTRONG

Horn of Plent

The Story of Louis Armstrong

ROBERT GOFFIN

THE SECOND LINE

Vol. XXIV   New Orleans Jazz Club   Summer, 1972

LOUIS ARMSTRONG MEMORIAL PARK
PLANNED FOR NEW ORLEANS
(Story on page five)

THE SECOND LINE, SUMMER, 1972

SWING THAT MUSIC

BY LOUIS ARMSTRONG

WITH SPECIAL EXAMPLES OF SWING MUSIC CONTRIBUTED BY
BENNY GOODMAN   JOE VENUTI
TOMMY DORSEY   BUD FREEMAN
RED NORVO   LOUIS ARMSTRONG
CLAUDE HOPKINS   CARL KRESS
STANLEY DENNIS   RAY BAUDUC
INTRODUCTION BY RUDY VALLEE

LOUIS

The Louis Armstrong Story

KINGS OF JAZZ

Louis Armstrong

JAZZ

NO. 10
BER. 1943

regards

DANS CE NUMÉRO:

LES VÉLIVOLES
A LA CONQUÊTE
DES NUAGES

★

GEORGES GUÉTARY
CHANTE A LONDRES

16e Année
N° 92
NOUVELLE SÉRIE
10 F
9 Mai
1947

PETIT FILS DE L'ONCLE TOM

LOUIS ARMST

Metronome

APRIL, 1945   25c
Thirty Cents in Canada

LOUIS

February, 1947

No. 52

"We had his photo pinned above our pillows, between the half-naked bimbos and the old saints. We stuck his face in our everyday notebooks. He gave comfort against our teachers, against our families.... He was with us in our reading, he reigned over our vacations."

Jacques Chessex

Trumpeter's Tale
THE STORY OF YOUNG LOUIS ARMSTRONG

Jeanette Eaton
illustrated by ELTON C. FAX

LOUIS
ARMSTRONG

Muvie
★

MA
NOUVELLE
ORLEANS

"A phonograph was playing low; it seemed infinite violins were accompanying the unique voice of Louis Armstrong, a rocky harmony striding down the mountainside, conjuring up memories of a pale moon shining through the trees, a steamboat sailing down the river."

David Goodis
Epaves

"He turned on the radio and played with the tuning dial until he found some music. Program of jazz recordings; he recognized the tune being played as Louis Armstrong's 'Four Or Five Times'. After that came other Hot Five classics of the twenties, 'Didn't He Ramble', 'Wish I Could Shimmy Like My Sister Kate', 'Jelly Roll', 'Beale Street Blues'. An all-Satchmo program!"

Bernard Wolfe
Limbo

he's going to send to you some
Red Beans + Rice — Gee — I wish
I were over there in Paris — so I could
cook them for you — and help you
eat them — Ha Ha — I personally
think — that is a real treat.
Am also sending a Diet Chart —
to you — In case you can't find
any Pluto Water over there —
Just get a bottle of Hunyardi
Water — That will serve the
same — Bob was just reading
your Book — Kings of Jazz and
12 years of Jazz — to me.
He Translated them for me.

"Together they went to see a student on the Place du Panthéon to listen to the Brandenburg Concertos and records by Armstrong. Germain talked about the torture. Stop it, said Duc, stop it, will you, listen to Armstrong!"

Roger Vailland
La Fête

"I had expressed a wish to hear some jazz music, and here I was en route to a Louis Armstrong concert at Carnegie Hall; a bit of luck, for it was years since Armstrong had made a concert appearance, and every seat had been booked a long time ahead. [...] Armstrong's appearance was greeted with frenzied applause; one again, I recognized the face I had seen in so many photographs..."

Simone de Beauvoir
L'Amérique au jour le jour

"...It was a record from old America. It was Louis Armstrong in a staggering break. Others had experienced the same joys with a woman glimpsed in the street, a painting seen in a museum. We were no less happy."

Jacques Bureau

Woody Allen in Manhattan (1979), enumerating "the things that make life worth living."

"[...] My eyes moist with joy, my nostrils ravished by restaurants, perfumed beauties and woods. My ears avid with Armstrong."

Gaston Criel

"At Odéon we have found a true masterpiece
that everyone should own. It is 'Exactly Like You',
by Louis Armstrong. It is heartrending. So much
sorrow and despair is overwhelming.
It is a sublime record."

Darius Milhaud

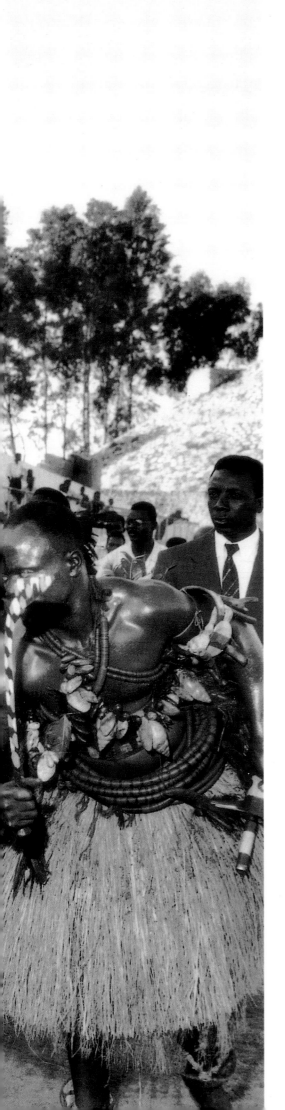

"People sometimes smile when we speak of negritude. Why not smile when you are speaking of bread and salt and milk, when you are speaking of earth and rivers and forests. For negritude is a rich earth, irrigated by rivers whose names are Nile, Congo and Zambeze, an earth of barbarous alluvia in which there grow deeply rooted virgin forests with tornadoes in their boughs. Louis Armstrong is a Negro and he expresses himself like a Negro, like old Africa. Watch him, for he dances, hear him. See, listen, he is raising his trumpet and making it growl like thunder, with the cataracts of the tornado or the murmur of springs. But if he can play like this with the most despotic laws of music, it is because his two feet are firmly planted on Mother Earth, like Antaeus. Because he rests on the basic rhythm of percussion instruments. As in Africa, the dancer who, his tom-tom under his arm, performs the most dazzling fantasies with counter-tempos and syncopations. If Louis Armstrong does it, if the African dancer does it, it is because they are sustained by a despotic rhythm, that of Mother Africa.

But Louis Armstrong also sings. In his voice animated by Cosmic Forces, in that voice that expresses all the elements, in that soft and gravelly, ironic and tender voice, we hear, in turn, thunder, tornado and sea on the rocks, the spring on the grass. The voice of the gorilla and the voice of the turtle dove. And that is why Louis Armstrong's trumpet, Louis Armstrong's voice, cannot be put on paper.

It is a trumpet, a voice beyond, or rather, before mathematics. It is the voice of the dawn of the world, the voice of God creating the world in modulated images, in rhythmic images."

Léopold Sédar Senghor

Louis at Leopoldville, Congo, 1960.

131

"Of all my joys, Armstrong's trumpet
Was the most sonorous and the most heartrending,
The echo has stayed with my nights, it sings,
Penetrates me, explodes my head,
Whispers in the depths of a dream of silence."

Franz Hellens

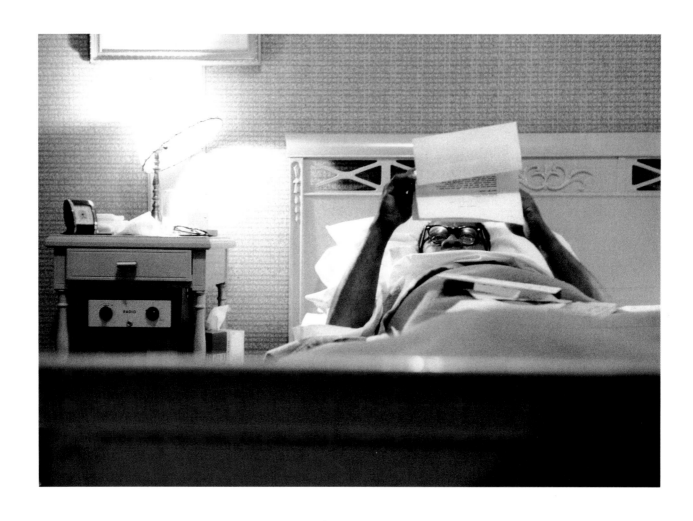

"Louis Armstrong: a poet whose attempt to express himself in words is shattered every time he tries because, in the end, poetry is unsayable. In his particular language, however, this poetry succeeds in touching the sensibility of individuals all over the globe and, what it loses of the magic of words, it gains in universality. I love this poetry because, thus transposed, it is spoken and refuses emphasis and declamation; and it is precisely for what it has to say, that it appears in the moving form of human truth, at once passion and depth."

Tristan Tzara

Louis and Guylaine Guy,
called 'princess of rhythm'.